聞いて覚える英単語
キクタン
TOEFL® TEST
【イディオム編】

TOEFL iBT®&TOEFL ITP®両対応

高橋基治／ロバート・ヒルキ／ポール・ワーデン著

アルク

英語は聞いて覚える！
アルク・キクタンシリーズ

「読む」だけでは、言葉は決して身につきません。私たちが日本語を習得できたのは、赤ちゃんのころから日本語を繰り返し「聞いて」きたから——『キクタン』シリーズは、この「当たり前のこと」にこだわり抜いた単語集・熟語集です。「読んでは忘れ、忘れては読む」——そんな悪循環とはもうサヨナラです。「聞いて覚える」、そして「読んで理解する」、さらに「使って磨く」——英語習得の「新しい1歩」が、この1冊から必ず始まります！

Preface
TOEFL スコアアップの鍵を握る 厳選イディオム 400 が効率的に身に付きます!

文　高橋基治

1日16イディオム、25日間で TOEFLハイスコアの土台を 確実に築く! 充実の演習問題で 復習も万全。

本書は、過去にアルクから出版された『TOEFL® テスト完全攻略　英熟語』を底本とし、聞いて覚える英単語「キクタンシリーズ」として再編されたものです。TOEFL でハイスコアを取るために特に重要なイディオム 400 が厳選されており、単語に焦点を当てた同シリーズの『TOEFL Test【頻出編】』と併せて学習すれば、単・熟語の対策は完璧です。

改編に際し、1 日の学習量を 16 イディオムに限定し、25 日で確実に覚えられるように再構成しています。効果的に「覚える」ためには「耳」からの学習は不可欠。そこで本書では、楽しい音楽に乗りながら耳からも語彙を定着させる「チャンツ CD」を 1 枚、さらに、学んだイディオムがきちんと身に付いているかを確認できる「チャレンジドリル 100」に対応した CD も 1 枚用意しています。

日常会話に頻出する イディオムなので、 留学後もずっと役立つ! 類義表現をマスターして アウトプット力も倍増。

本書では、過去実際に登場した、あるいは今後も登場しそうなイディオムばかりを出来得る限り数多く掲載しています。さらには、留学後も現地での日常生活にも役立つよう、慣用句・ことわざ・口語表現といった類まで含めてあります。従って、日常会話で使う言い回しを押さえたいと願う学習者にとっても、絶好のトレーニング教材であるといえます。

そして、それぞれのイディオムについて、その類義表現も身に付くように配慮しています。英語は、ある表現を別の表現に言い変えていく（パラフレーズする）ことの多い言語です。類義表現を覚えておくことで、イディオムの意味をより正確に理解できるようになるばかりか、リーディングやリスニングが楽になり、さらに自らのライティングやスピーキングにも活かせるようになるのです。

Contents

1日16イディオム、25日間で TOEFL®必須400表現を完全マスター

【記号説明】

CD-A1

CD-A のトラック 1 です。

CD-A1 (continued)

CD-A1 の続きです。

・(　)：省略可能を表す。
例) get through (to ～)
(～に) 電話が通じる
・[　]：言い換え可能を表す。
例) heads or [nor] tails
※or の代わりに nor でも良い、の意。
・〈　〉：補足説明を表す。
例) spell out ～
～を〈詳細に〉説明する
・～：名詞・名詞節を表す。
・≒：類義表現を表す。
・A、B：名詞を表す。
・doing：動名詞を表す。
・one's、oneself：それぞれ、名詞・代名詞の所有格、再帰代名詞を表す。

「動詞＋副詞＋名詞」の形を取るイディオムについて、名詞に当たる個所が代名詞でない場合、以下のように語の入れ替えが可能です。
例) put off ～
○) put off a trip / put a trip off / put it off
×) put off it

TOEFL® テストとは

TOEFL テストとは

TOEFL（Test of English as a Foreign Language）テストとは、その名称が示すように、外国語としての英語力判定テストである。アメリカの非営利教育団体 Educational Testing Service（ETS）により開発運営されている TOEFL テストは、主にアメリカやカナダの大学院、大学・短大で、留学志願者の英語力が授業についていくのに必要な基準に達しているかを測るための目安として使われてきた。最近では、アメリカ、カナダのみならずイギリス、オーストラリア、ニュージーランドを含む英語圏各国において、8500 を超える大学・短大が、英語が母語でない留学生に対して、必要な英語力の基準を、TOEFL テストのスコアで提示し、入学要件のひとつとしている（TOEFL テストとともに他の英語力判定テストのスコアを採用している大学もある）。現在では、インターネットを利用して行われる Internet-Based Testing（以下 iBT）と呼ばれる TOEFL テストが実施されており、従来の Paper-Based Testing（PBT）はすでに中止されている（便宜的に実施される可能性はある）。

TOEFL iBT の概要

TOEFL iBT は、リーディング、リスニング、スピーキング、ライティングの 4 つのセクションに分かれている。リーディングとリスニングは選択式で、選択肢や文中の語などをマウスでクリックする解答方式となっている。スピーキングは設問に対する自分の考えを述べたり、提示される内容を要約して話したりする方式で、ライティングはタイピングによって解答する。テスト時間の合計は約 4 時間半、問題数合計は Pretest（採点されないといわれている設問）が含まれるため 78 ～ 129問となっている。各セクションでメモを取ることが許されている。

〈リーディングセクション〉（試験時間:60〜100分／問題数:36〜70問）

3〜5つのパッセージを読み設問に答えるセクション。このセクションでは1パッセージ約700語の文章を20分程度で読む必要があるので、かなりの速読能力が求められる。出題範囲が広いため、普段からさまざまな分野のトピックやニュースを英語で読んでおくことが重要である。

〈リスニングセクション〉（試験時間：60〜90分／問題数：34〜51問）

2〜3つの会話、4〜6つの講義や討論を聞き設問に答えるセクション。このセクションでは「適切なメモを取る力」と「高度なリスニング能力」が求められる。会議や講義、討論は非常に長いので、ポイントを押さえたメモをとる練習が必要となる。

〈スピーキングセクション〉（試験時間：20分／問題数：6タスク）

受験者はマイク付ヘッドセットをつけ、パソコン画面に表示されるタスクに対してマイクを通して英語で解答する。1つのタスクにつき、解答時間は45〜60秒。短時間で思考をまとめ、論理的にスピーチを行う能力が求められるので、日頃からスピーチの練習をしておく必要がある。

〈ライティングセクション〉（試験時間：50分／問題数：2タスク）

3分間でパッセージを読み、その後2分程度の短い講義を聞いて設問に答える統合型問題（Integrated Task）と、あるトピックについての意見をまとめる形式の問題（Independent Task）とが出題される。正しい文法の知識、文章構成能力、タイピング技術はもちろん、統合型問題では読解力、リスニング能力も求められる。

TOEFL ITPとは

TOEFL ITP（Institutional Testing Program）は、TOEFLテスト作成・運営元であるETSが提供するTOEFLの団体向けテストプログラムのことである。主に教育機関において大学・短大、高校でのクラス分けや大学院入試などに利用されている。交換留学の選考で求められることも多いが、TOEFL ITPスコアは試験実施団体内でのみ有効で、公的には認められない。そのため交換留学以外で留学を希望する場合は、本試験として実施されるTOEFL iBTを受験する必要がある。

問題は2種類ある。ひとつはTOEFL PBTで過去に出題された試験問題を再利用して出題されるLevel 1 TOEFL、もうひとつはLevel 1 TOEFLの難易度を下げたLevel 2 Pre-TOEFLである。本書ではLevel 1 TOEFLを対象としている。試験内容は、リスニング、文法、リーディングの3つのセクションから成り、TOEFL iBTで実施されるライティング、スピーキングセクションは出題されない。すべて4者択一の試験問題で解答はマークシート方式。メモをとることは禁止されている。

〈リスニングセクション〉（試験時間：約35分／問題数：50問）

短い会話、長い会話、講義の一部などを聞き、その内容に関する設問に答えるセクション。短い会話は10、長い会話は2つ、講義の一部などは3つ読まれ、それぞれに対して30問、8問、12問が出題される。

〈文法セクション〉（試験時間：25分／問題数：40問）

英文の空所に適切な語句を補充するStructureと、英文中の間違いを指摘するWritten Expressionが出題される。問題数はそれぞれ15問と25問。

〈リーディングセクション〉（試験時間：55分／問題数：50問）

200～300語程度の英文を読み、その内容および本文中の語彙に関する設問に答えるセクション。出題される英文は5つ程度。

スコアについて

TOEFL iBTのスコアは、リーディング、リスニング、スピーキング、ライティングの4つのセクション別に0～30点の間で算出され、その合計が全体のスコアとなる。つまり最低スコアが0点、最高スコアは120点となる。TOEFL ITPでは、リスニング、文法、リーディングの全セクションの合計スコアは、最高677、最低310。セクションごとに、正解数を基にしたスコアが換算表（非公開）で算出される。それらを合計して10を掛け、3で割った数が全体のスコアになる。

TOEFLテストのスコアは英語圏の多くの大学で英語力の判定材料とされ、大学、短大によって要求されるスコアは異なる。目安として、アメリカの場合、コミュニティーカレッジと呼ばれる2年制大学ではTOEFL iBTで46～61、TOEFL ITPで450～500、学部留学ではiBT：61～80、ITP：500～550、大学院留学ではiBT：80～100、ITP：550～600が目標とされている。しかし入学のための競

【iBT／ITPテストスコア換算表】

iBT	120	105	100	93	89	80	68	61	46	32	0-8
ITP	677	620	600	580	570	550	520	500	450	400	310

争が激しい学校や、高い英語能力が要求される専攻分野などでは、要求スコアがこの目安よりも高めに設定されている場合がある。

受験手続きについて

TOEFL ITPは団体が実施する試験であるため、個人での受験申込みはできない。ここでは、一般に公開されているTOEFL iBTの受験手続きの方法を紹介する。
まず、Information and Registration Bulletin（以下Bulletin）と呼ばれる受験要項を入手する。Bulletinには、受験手続きから教材の購入方法まで、TOEFLテストに関する諸注意が詳細に説明されている。情報のほとんどが英語で書かれているため、全部を読みこなすのは大変だが、TOEFLテスト受験の第一歩と考え挑戦してみよう。Bulletinは、国際教育交換協議会（CIEE）日本代表部のウェブサイト、あるいは、日本でETSの代行をしているプロメトリック株式会社のウェブサイト、ETSが提供するTOEFLテストの公式サイトからダウンロードできる。次に、TOEFLテスト公式サイトで個人のアカウントページを作成し、受験の申し込み手続きをする。これはインターネットもしくは電話で申し込む際には必須となっている。
郵送で申し込む場合は、Bulletinに添付されている4ページからなる申込書（TOEFL Internet-based Test Registration Form）への記入が必要だ。その後、記入済み申込書と受験料210ドル（国際郵便為替、送金小切手、クレジットカードの場合はカード番号を記入）を、第1希望テスト日の4週間前必着でプロメトリック株式会社宛に送付すればよい。

【Bulletinの入手先（インターネット）】
国際教育交換協議会（CIEE）日本代表部
URL: http://www.cieej.or.jp/

プロメトリック株式会社
URL: http://www.prometric-jp.com/

ETS TOEFL公式サイト
URL: http://www.ets.org/toefl/

【テストの申込み先（郵送）】
プロメトリック株式会社 RRC予約センター
〒104-0033　東京都中央区新川1-21-2 茅場町タワー15F
プロメトリック株式会社 TOEFL iBT係

上記の情報はすべて2011年9月現在のもので、随時変更になる場合があります。

だから「ゼッタイに覚えられる」！

本書の構成

Chapter 1 ～ 3

CD-A 対応

本書では、過去に出題されたTOEFLテストの問題を調査し、日本人受験者にとって意味がつかみにくい一方で必ずマスターしておきたいイディオム400を精選しています。紹介する表現は、TOEFL、TOEICテスト研究の第一人者であるロバート・ヒルキ氏独自の分析結果を参考にしつつ、重要度別に3つのChapterに分けて掲載しています。

Chapter 1
（最頻出イディオム240）

重要度が最も高いもので、かつ特にnon-nativeにわかりづらいもの

Chapter 2
（頻出イディオム80）

重要度が高く、non-nativeにわかりづらいもの

Chapter 3
（重要イディオム80）

重要度はそれほど高くないが、ぜひ押さえておきたいもの

また、Chapter1ではDayが5つ終わるごとに、Chapter 2、3ではそれぞれのチャプターの終わりに、学んだイディオムをおさらいする**復習テスト**を用意してあります。復習テストには2種類の形式があり、両方の問題をこなすことで、すべてのイディオムの復習ができる仕組みになっています。

1

日本語の選択肢の中から、ふさわしい意味を表すものを見つける問題
⇒日本語でイディオムの持つイメージをつかむ。

2

英語の選択肢の中から、ふさわしい意味を表すものを見つける問題
⇒イディオムに込められた、日本語訳からはつかみにくいニュアンスを理解する。

本書は、TOEFL テストで高得点を取るためには不可欠かつ、英語圏の日常会話にも頻出するイディオム 400 が、無理なく身につくように工夫された一冊です。

Chapter 4

CD-B 対応

本書の締めくくりとして、CD の音声を聞いて答える問題を合計100題用意しています。問題形式は 2 種類あります。

1

イディオムを含む文を聞き取り、空所に適切な語句を埋める問題(空所補充問題)
⇒イディオムを理解するに当たり、イディオムを含んだ発言を確実に聞き取る練習をする。

2

イディオムを含んだ会話を聞き、質問に答える問題（選択肢問題）
⇒ TOEFL ITP のリスニングセクション Part A と同形式（ただし、「速聴・速解」の訓練のため、問題の間隔を実際［12秒］より少し短め［10秒］に設定)。実践の場に近い形での理解力を確かめる。

付属CDについて

●弊社制作の音声 CD は、CD プレーヤーでの再生を保証する規格品です。

●パソコンでご使用になる場合、CD-ROM ドライブとの相性により、ディスクを再生できない場合がございます。ご了承ください。

●パソコンでタイトル・トラック情報を表示させたい場合は、iTunes をご利用ください。iTunes では、弊社が CD のタイトル・トラック情報を登録している Gracenote 社の CDDB（データベース）からインターネットを介してトラック情報を取得することができます。

● CD として正常に音声が再生できるディスクからパソコンや mp3 プレーヤー等への取り込み時にトラブルが生じた際は、まず、そのアプリケーション(ソフト)、プレーヤーの製作元へご相談ください。

目と耳をフル活用

本書とCDの利用法

本書…

見出しイディオム

1日の学習イディオム数は16です。見開きの左側に学習イディオムが掲載されています。CDでは、上から順にイディオムが登場します。最初の8つが流れたら、ページをめくって次の8つに進みましょう。

意味・類義表現

見出しイディオムの意味です。代表的な意味を色付きの太字にし、CDに収録しています。類義表現を併せて掲載しているので、イディオムのニュアンスをつかむのに役立てることができます。

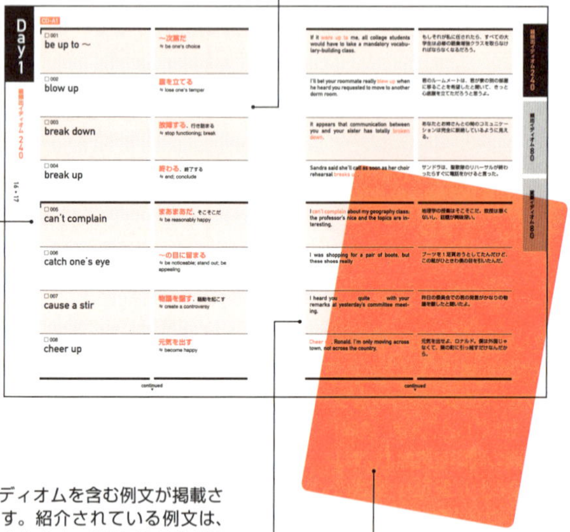

例文

見出しイディオムを含む例文が掲載されています。紹介されている例文は、TOEFLのみならず、英語圏の日常生活でも役に立つものばかりなので、例文の中で使い方をしっかり確認しておきましょう。

チェックシート

チェックシートは復習に活用してください。見開きの左側では、イディオムを見てその意味がすぐにわかるか、右側では、訳を参考に隠されている表現が思い浮かべられるかを確認しましょう。

CD… 本書には、CD が 2 枚付属しています。目で見て覚えるだけでなく、耳で聞いて覚え、さらに問題演習を経ることで、イディオムを一層確実に定着させることができます。

CD-A

Chapter 1 ～ 3 の見出しイディオム 400 が「英→日→英→ポーズ」の順に収録されています（例文および復習テストの音声は収められていません）。該当する CD トラックを呼び出してチャンツを聞き、見出しイディオムの発音と意味を一緒に覚えましょう。

TIPS! 毎日のちょっとした空き時間を利用して繰り返しCDを聞くことで、英語のリズムやリスニング力が身に付きます。慣れてきたら、本を見ずにCDを聞き、ポーズで英語を発音しましょう。

CD-B

Chapter 4 の問題音声が収録されています。チャレンジドリルは、空所補充問題（イディオムを聞き取って空所を埋める）と選択肢問題（イディオムを含んだ会話を聞いて答える）で構成されています。共に、問題間には10秒間のポーズが入っています。

TIPS! CDは、問題を解くためだけに使うのではなく、流れてくる英文を書き取ってみたり（dictation）、ナレーターに続けて繰り返して言ってみたりする（shadowing）と良いでしょう。

例文の音声をインターネットでダウンロード購入できます！

英語オーディオブック（http://www.alc.co.jp/book/onsei-dl/）
▶▶ アルクのデジタルコンテンツ ▶▶ 商品カテゴリ：留学 TOEFL
▶▶「キクタン TOEFL イディオム編：例文音声」にアクセス！

iTunes Store（オーディオブック）、MORA［モーラ］、楽天ダウンロードなど、お好きなダウンロードサイトよりお求めください。

※各ダウンロードサイトにより、音声の形式、再生可能なプレイヤーが異なりますので、事前にご確認ください。

Chapter 1
最頻出
イディオム
240

CD-A1

□001 **be up to ～**	**～次第だ** ≒ be one's choice
□002 **blow up**	**腹を立てる** ≒ lose one's temper
□003 **break down**	**故障する**、行き詰まる ≒ stop functioning; break
□004 **break up**	**終わる**、終了する ≒ end; conclude
□005 **can't complain**	**まあまあだ**、そこそこだ ≒ be reasonably happy
□006 **catch one's eye**	**～の目に留まる** ≒ be noticeable; stand out; be appealing
□007 **cause a stir**	**物議を醸す**、騒動を起こす ≒ create a controversy
□008 **cheer up**	**元気を出す** ≒ become happy

continued ▼

If it were up to me, all college students would have to take a mandatory vocabulary-building class.	もしそれが私に任されたら、すべての大学生は必修の語彙増強クラスを取らなければならなくなるだろう。
I'll bet your roommate really blew up when he heard you requested to move to another dorm room.	君のルームメートは、君が寮の別の部屋に移ることを希望したと聞いて、きっと心底腹を立てただろうと思うよ。
It appears that communication between you and your sister has totally broken down.	あなたとお姉さんとの間のコミュニケーションは完全に断絶しているように見える。
Sandra said she'll call as soon as her choir rehearsal breaks up.	サンドラは、聖歌隊のリハーサルが終わったらすぐに電話をかけると言った。
I can't complain about my geography class; the professor's nice and the topics are interesting.	地理学の授業はそこそこだ。教授は悪くないし、話題が興味深い。
I was shopping for a pair of boots, but these shoes really caught my eye.	ブーツを1足買おうとしてたんだけど、この靴がひときわ僕の目を引いたんだ。
I heard you caused quite a stir with your remarks at yesterday's committee meeting.	昨日の委員会での君の発言がかなりの物議を醸したと聞いたよ。
Cheer up, Ronald. I'm only moving across town, not across the country.	元気を出せよ、ロナルド。僕は外国じゃなくて、隣の町に引っ越すだけなんだから。

continued ▼

CD-A1 (continued)

□009 **come in handy**	**役に立つ** ≒ be useful
□010 **end up doing**	**～する羽目になる** ≒ eventually have to do
□011 **get around**	**動き回る**、歩き回る ≒ move from one place to another
□012 **hit it off**	**仲良くなる**、意気投合する ≒ start a relationship
□013 **hit the spot**	〈飲食物が〉**必要を満足させる**、申し分ない ≒ be refreshing; make one feel satisfied
□014 **hold off**	**先に延ばす**、遅らせる ≒ delay
□015 **jump the gun**	**先走る**、早まったことをする ≒ act prematurely
□016 **raise the roof**	**大騒ぎする** ≒ be extremely noisy

That new calendar you gave me sure has come in handy.

君がくれた新しいカレンダーは、本当に役に立った。

Karen missed the last train and ended up taking a taxi home.

カレンは終電に乗り遅れて、タクシーで家に帰る羽目になった。

New York is really crowded, but at least it's easy to get around there.

ニューヨークは本当に人が多いけれど、少なくともあちこち移動しやすい。

Vickie seems to have really hit it off with that guy she met at last week's party.

ビッキーは、先週のパーティーで知り合ったその男性と本当に仲良くなったようだ。

Nothing hits the spot like a cold glass of beer after playing basketball all afternoon.

午後ずっとバスケットボールをやった後の1杯の冷たいビールほど、爽快にさせてくれるものはない。

I'd like to hold off for at least a week before I make a final decision.

最終決断をする前に、少なくともあと1週間は猶予を取りたい。

Be careful not to jump the gun by announcing your candidacy too early. You don't want people to think you're too eager to be elected.

君の立候補をあまりに早く発表するなんて先走ったことのないように注意してね。選ばれるために気負い過ぎていると思われたくないでしょ。

The crowd at the hockey game really raised the roof when their team scored the final goal.

そのホッケーの試合での観衆は、応援するチームが決勝点を決めた時、ものすごい大騒ぎをした。

CD-A2

□017 **couldn't be better**	**最高である** ≒ be going very well
□018 **cut corners**	**手を抜く**、〈お金・時間・労力などを〉切り詰める ≒ not follow the correct procedures
□019 **eat out**	**外食する** ≒ eat in a restaurant
□020 **fall behind**	**遅れる** ≒ fail to keep up
□021 **fall through**	**失敗に終わる**、駄目になる ≒ be unexpectedly canceled
□022 **get along** (with ～)	(～と)**うまくやる**、(～と)付き合う ≒ have good relations (with ～)
□023 **get lost**	**消えうせる**、邪魔する ・命令の文脈で用いられる。 ≒ go away
□024 **get nowhere** (with ～)	(～〈物事〉が)**進展しない**、(～〈人〉とは)らちが明かない ≒ make no progress (with ～)

continued ▼

Things couldn't be better at work. My new boss is the best I've ever had.	職場の状況は最高だ。新しい上司は今までで一番いい。
The reason the apartment building collapsed during the earthquake is because the contractor cut corners with the materials used during construction.	地震でアパートが崩壊した原因だが、請負業者が建設に使用した資材に手を抜いたからだ。
If it's OK with you, let's eat out tonight. I didn't have time to go shopping for dinner.	もしよければ今夜は外食しようよ。夕食の買い物に行く時間がなかったんだ。
Al fell behind in his work early in the term and hasn't been able to catch up ever since.	アルは学期が始まって間もなく勉強で後れを取ってしまい、それ以来追いつくことができずにいる。
Tony was supposed to have a research grant to go abroad this summer, but it fell through at the last minute.	トニーはこの夏海外に行くための研究助成金をもらうことになっていたが、直前で駄目になった。
I hear you and your sister haven't been getting along so well recently.	近ごろ、君たち姉妹はあまりうまくいっていないと聞いている。
Paul told me to get lost when I asked if he'd like to have dinner with me this weekend.	私が、今週末一緒に夕食でもどうかと聞いたら、ポールは、あっちへ行けと言ったんだ。
I'm getting nowhere with my boss; he doesn't even seem to listen to what I say.	上司とはらちが明かない。彼は私の言うことを聞いてさえいないみたいだ。

continued ▼

CD-A2 (continued)

□ 025 **get through** (to ～)	(～に) **電話が通じる** ≒ reach (～) by phone
□ 026 **give in**	**屈する**、折れる ≒ yield
□ 027 **keep to oneself**	**人付き合いを避ける**、内向的である ≒ be introverted
□ 028 **lag behind**	**遅れる** ≒ fail to keep pace
□ 029 **slip one's mind**	**度忘れする** ≒ be forgotten
□ 030 **stand out**	**目立つ**、傑出する ≒ be unique; be visible [noticeable]
□ 031 **take it easy**	**気楽にやる**、落ち着く ≒ relax
□ 032 **turn up**	**姿を現す**、到着する ≒ appear; arrive

I've been trying to get through to Frank all day, but he hasn't been answering.

1日中フランクに電話が通じるかかけてみたが、彼は電話に出なかった。

If you're really serious about losing weight, Arthur, you can't keep giving in to the temptation to snack between meals.

もしあなたが本当に体重を減らすことに真剣なら、アーサー、間食の誘惑に負けてばかりではいけないよ。

Alice basically keeps to herself, but it's probably just because she's shy, not because she's unfriendly.

アリスは基本的には人付き合いを避けているが、たぶんただ恥ずかしがりなだけで、愛想がないからではない。

Jerry is lagging behind in his physics class; he's only done half of the lab work.

ジェリーは、物理の授業で遅れている。実験の作業が半分しか終わってないんだ。

It totally slipped my mind that today was your birthday.

今日が君の誕生日だということを、完璧に度忘れしていたよ。

You'd never even notice him in class, but his written work really stands out.

授業の中では彼に気付きさえしないだろうが、彼の作文は非常に際立っている。

Your work has been very stressful this past month. I strongly recommend that you take it easy for a few days.

あなたの仕事は、このひと月の間とても大変でしたね。数日間は気楽にやることを強くお勧めします。

I hope my wallet turns up soon; all my credit cards were in it.

財布が早く見つかればいいのに。クレジットカードが中にすべて入っていたんだ。

CD-A3

□ 033 **bury the hatchet**	**仲直りする** ≒ agree to stop fighting
□ 034 **catch on**	**はやる**、人気を博する ≒ become popular
□ 035 **get together**	**集まる**、会う ≒ meet
□ 036 **give credibility** (to ～)	(～を)**信用する**、(～を)信頼する ≒ put faith (in ～)
□ 037 **go ahead**	**進める**、どうぞ ≒ proceed; begin to do
□ 038 **go Dutch**	**割り勘にする** ≒ pay equally
□ 039 **go overboard**	**度を超す** ≒ go to extremes
□ 040 **have a flat** (tire)	**パンクする** ≒ get a punctured tire

continued ▼

Why don't you and Martha bury the hatchet? You two have more in common than either of you admit.	マーサと仲直りをしたらどうなの？　君たち２人は、自分たちが認めている以上に共通点が多いんだよ。
If your new product catches on, you'll be so rich you won't know what to do with all your money.	もし新製品がはやったら、あなたは自分のお金の使い道がわからなくなるくらいの大金持ちになるだろう。
If it's convenient for you, we can get together Friday to discuss the Barton contract.	もし君の都合がつけばだけど、バートン社との契約について話し合うために金曜日に集まれるよ。
I'd be wary about giving too much credibility to anything Roger says about politics; he's usually just talking through his hat.	政治についてロジャーが話すことを信用し過ぎないよう用心しなくては。彼はたいていいい加減なことしか言わないから。
Since Bob is running late, let's go ahead with the meeting anyway.	ボブは遅れているのだから、ともかく会議を進めましょう。
What do you say we go Dutch for our date this Friday? It's not fair that you should pay every time.	今度の金曜日のデートは割り勘にしない？　君が毎回払うのはフェアじゃないよ。
If you wouldn't go overboard every time you went shopping, you might be able to save a few dollars at the end of the month.	もし買い物のたびに無駄遣いをしなければ、月末には数ドル節約することができるかもしれない。
What a bad time to have a flat! I'm supposed to be at the dentist's in five minutes.	こんなときにパンクするなんて！　５分後には歯医者にいる予定なのに。

continued
▼

CD-A3 (continued)

□ 041 **hit the books**	**勉強する** ≒ study
□ 042 **kick off**	**始まる** ≒ begin
□ 043 **knock it off**	**やめる** ・通常命令・依頼の文脈で用いられる。 ≒ stop doing [saying] it
□ 044 **make waves**	**波風を立てる** ≒ cause minor conflicts
□ 045 **pull one's leg**	**～をからかう**、～をかつぐ ≒ joke; tease
□ 046 **push one's luck**	**図に乗る**、悪乗りする ≒ go too far; tempt fate
□ 047 **split the bill**	**割り勘にする** ≒ divide the cost
□ 048 **stay up**	**寝ずに起きている** ≒ remain awake

Our final exam is in two weeks. I'd better hit the books now.

期末試験は２週間後だ。もう勉強した方がいいね。

What time does the dorm dance kick off?

寮のダンスは何時に始まるの？

Knock it off, would you? I'm trying to study.

やめてくれませんか。勉強しようとしているんです。

Your new work situation may be unfair, but I suggest you not make any waves until you've been there a little longer.

新しい仕事環境は不当かもしれないが、もうしばらくそこにいるうちは波風を立てないことを勧めるよ。

She doesn't mean that, Fred; she's just pulling your leg.

そういうつもりじゃないよ、フレッド。彼女はただ君をからかってるだけなんだ。

You've been pushing your luck by not turning in your homework on time.

君は図に乗って、期限通りに宿題を出さずにきている。

I won't let you pay for the whole meal; I insist we split the bill equally.

君に食事代を全部支払わせるつもりはないよ。平等に割り勘にしよう。

It was already 4 a.m., so rather than sleep only two hours, I just stayed up.

もう午前４時だった。だから２時間だけ眠るというのはやめて、ただ寝ずに起きていた。

CD-A4

□ 049
bank on ～

～を当てにする
≒ rely on ～ ; depend on ～

□ 050
be onto ～

～をつかんでいる、～に感づいている
≒ be discovering ～

□ 051
be sold out

売り切れである
≒ have all been bought

□ 052
chip in ～

～をカンパする、～を寄付する
≒ contribute

□ 053
come down with ～

～〈病気〉にかかる
≒ catch <an illness>

□ 054
figure out ～

〈考えた末〉**～がわかる**
≒ understand

□ 055
go over ～

～を復習する、～を検討する
≒ review

□ 056
keep clear of ～

～を避ける、～を敬遠する
≒ avoid

continued ▼

I know I haven't always turned my work in on time in the past, Professor Kennedy, but you can bank on me to submit everything promptly from now on.

私が今までいつも遅れずに課題を提出していたわけではないことはわかっています、ケネディー教授、ですが、今からはすべてを遅れることなく提出するので期待してください。

Linda and her research team may really be onto something exciting with their new discoveries about DNA.

リンダと調査班はDNAに関する彼らの新しい発見で、実は、驚くべき何かをつかんでいるかもしれない。

The tickets for the Broadway production are completely sold out; they don't even have standing-room-only ones left.

ブロードウェー上演のチケットは完売した。立見席のチケットさえ残っていない。

If we all chip in a few dollars, we can order a pizza to be delivered to our dorm.

全員で数ドルずつカンパすれば、寮にピザの出前を取ることができる。

I feel terrible; I think I may be coming down with something.

具合が悪いな。何かの病気にかかっているのかもしれない。

I can't figure out this math problem, can you?

僕はこの数学の問題がわからないんだけど、君は？

I only have five minutes to go over the handouts for the meeting.

会議のための配布物を見直すのに、5分しか時間がない。

Keep clear of Wilshire Boulevard this morning; there's been a terrible accident.

けさはウィルシャー大通りを使うのはやめてくれ。ひどい事故があったんだ。

continued ▼

CD-A4(continued)

□ 057 **learn the ropes**	〈仕事などの〉**コツを覚える** ≒ learn the basics
□ 058 **make no difference**	**どちらでもよい**、関係ない ≒ be of no consequence
□ 059 **make sense**	**意味を成す**、理解できる ≒ seem understandable [comprehensive]
□ 060 **show up**	**姿を現す** ≒ arrive
□ 061 **sort out ～**	**～を解決する**、～を片付ける ≒ resolve
□ 062 **stand up for ～**	**～を支持する**、～を擁護する ≒ defend
□ 063 **take a shortcut**	**近道する** ≒ take a shorter route
□ 064 **wrap up ～**	**～を終える** ≒ complete

Once Alan learns the ropes, he'll make a fine secretary.

アランは一度コツを覚えれば、立派な秘書になるだろう。

It makes no difference whether you like the new rules or not; you have to obey them.

その新しい規則が気に入るか入らないかは関係ない。君は、それに従わなければならないんだ。

Does this map make any sense to you? I haven't got a clue.

この地図があなたには理解できますか。私にはさっぱりわかりません。

What time should I show up for dance practice?

ダンスの練習には何時に行けばいいですか。

Mark's going to take a semester off to try to sort out some of the personal problems he's been having.

マークは、ずっと抱えている個人的な問題をいくつか片づけようと1学期休むつもりだ。

If you stand up for what you believe in, people will respect you more.

もし君が自らの信じるものを大切にすれば、人々はもっと敬意を払うだろう。

Let's take a shortcut, so that we can save some time.

近道をしよう、そうすればいくらか時間を節約できるから。

Let's wrap up this last chapter and then we can all go home.

この最後の章を終わらせれば、みんな家に帰れる。

CD-A5

□ 065 **call off ～**	**～を中止する** ≒ cancel
□ 066 **chew out ～**	**～をこっぴどくしかる** ≒ angrily reprimand [chastise]
□ 067 **come up with ～**	**～を思い付く**、～を考え付く ≒ find
□ 068 **count on ～**	**～に頼る**、～を当てにする ≒ rely upon ～
□ 069 **cut down on ～**	**～**〈出費・数量など〉**を抑える**、～を控える ≒ reduce
□ 070 **cut out ～**	**～を取り除く** • Cut it [that] out. で「やめろ、よせ、黙れ」の意。 ≒ remove
□ 071 **drop by ～**	**～に立ち寄る** ≒ drop in to ～; stop by ～
□ 072 **get at ～**	**～を言おうとする**、～をほのめかす ≒ imply

continued ▼

I'm actually happy the field trip was called off; now I'll have time to finish my term paper.	現地調査旅行が中止になって実はうれしい。おかげで、学期末リポートを仕上げる時間ができる。
My father chewed me out for coming home so late last night.	ゆうべ帰宅がとても遅かったので、父にこっぴどくしかられた。
How are you planning to come up with a location for our class trip this summer?	この夏の修学旅行の場所をどのように考えて決めるつもりですか。
It was a terrible mistake to count on Melvin to prepare the refreshments for the party.	パーティーの軽食の準備をメルビンに頼ったのは、大間違いだった。
I'm trying to lose weight by cutting down on the number of sodas I drink in a day.	僕は、1日に飲む炭酸飲料の数を抑えることで、減量しようとしているんだ。
I wish you'd cut out the extra information and make your point clearer.	余分な情報を省いて要点をもっと明快にすればいいと思うんだけどなあ。
Jeff, I'd appreciate it if you'd drop by my office later in the day.	ジェフ、後で会社にちょっと立ち寄ってもらえるとありがたいんだけど。
I'm afraid I don't really see what it is that you're getting at, Janet. Could you be a little more specific?	申し訳ありませんが、何をおっしゃりたいのかよくわかりません、ジャネット。もう少し具体的に話していただけませんか。

continued ▼

CD-A5(continued)

□073 **get over ～**	**～を克服する**、～から回復する ≒ recover from ～
□074 **give ～ a hand**	**～に手を貸す** ≒ help
□075 **kick around ～**	**～**〈計画・問題など〉**について話し合う** ≒ discuss
□076 **let off ～**	**～**〈人〉**を**〈乗り物から〉**降ろす** ≒ drop off ～; let out ～
□077 **live up to ～**	**～**〈期待など〉**に応える** ≒ meet one's standards
□078 **put off ～**	**～を延期する** ≒ delay; postpone
□079 **put up with ～**	**～を我慢する**、～に耐える ≒ tolerate; endure
□080 **turn down ～**	**～を却下する**、～を断る ≒ reject

Michelle still hasn't gotten over the fact that she didn't win the speech contest.

ミシェルは、スピーチコンテストで優勝できなかったという事実からまだ立ち直っていない。

Could you give me a hand carrying this furniture upstairs to my new apartment?

新しいアパートの２階にこの家具を運ぶのに手を貸してもらえますか。

Can we meet Monday to kick around the new budget proposal?

月曜日に会って、新しい予算案について話し合えませんか。

Do you mind letting me off in front of the market? I need to do some shopping.

スーパーの前で降ろしてもらえるかい？買い物しなくちゃいけないんだ。

Unfortunately, the new secretary hasn't lived up to anyone's expectations.

不運にも、新しい秘書は誰の期待にも応えられなかった。

Ken's motto seems to be, "Never do today that which you can put off until tomorrow."

ケンのモットーは、「明日に延期できることは決して今日やるな」であるようだ。

Greg said he can't put up with his roommate's snoring any longer.

グレッグは、ルームメートのいびきにもうこれ以上我慢できないと言った。

Did you really turn down that marketing job offer you got?

あのマーケティングの仕事の申し出を本当に断わったの？

復習テスト（Day 1-5）

（正解・訳例は pp.46-47）

1 赤字の意味としてもっともふさわしいものを A ～ D の中から選びなさい。

1. "Professor Graham, would it be all right to change the topic of my paper?"
"Yes, it's totally up to you."

A. あなたには早い B. あなた次第だ C. あなたには無理だ D. あなたなら大丈夫だ

2. On the way back home from school my car broke down in the middle of nowhere.

A. ペチャンコになった B. 故障した C. ガソリンがなくなった D. 衝突した

3. After midnight, the admissions committee meeting finally broke up.

A. 延長された B. 始まった C. 終わった D. 行き詰まった

4. "How's the new apartment you moved into last week?" "Well, I can't complain."

A. まあまあだね B. 困っている C. 絶望だ D. 言葉を失うよ

5. Abby was the first person to catch my eye at the party.

A. じろじろ見る B. 見守る C. 夢中になる D. 目に留まる

6. Kenny always ends up causing a stir by being such a rumor monger.

A. もめ事を起こす　B. ノイローゼになる　C. 嫌われる　D. あこがれの的になる

7. When I feel miserable, mountain climbing usually helps me cheer up.

A. 応援する　B. 鍛錬する　C. 元気が出る　D. 目が覚める

8. Why don't you take your coat with you? It'll come in handy if it rains.

A. 手に入る　B. 似合う　C. 役に立つ　D. 手ごろな値段になる

9. "I heard you started working out at the gym regularly. How's it going?"
"Couldn't be better, Rick!"

A. まあまあだよ　B. 最悪だよ　C. 絶好調だよ　D. まだわからないよ

10. The building contractor was severely criticized for the way he cut corners on the new skyscraper downtown.

A. 手を抜く　B. 作業を中断する　C. 工期を延ばす　D. わいろを渡す

11. Since I'm getting by on a scholarship, it's not financially wise for me to eat out every day.

A. 腹いっぱい食べる　B. 外食する　C. 偏食する　D. 貯金を食いつぶす

12. Our competition is falling behind in the area of computer engineering.

A. 失敗を犯す B. 後れを取る C. 協力する D. 追いつかれる

13. The party fell through when the guest of honor said she couldn't attend.

A. 無理に続けられた B. 次回に持ち越された C. 実現されなかった D. 規模が小さくなった

14. Sue may be pretty smart, but she's a difficult woman to get along with.

A. 結婚する B. 理解する C. 付き合う D. 我慢する

15. Even after a three-hour discussion, we still got nowhere trying to set next year's budget.

A. あいまいに決着した B. 無難に落ち着いた C. 先延ばしになった D. 進展がなかった

16. I've been trying to call Kim and Ellen since this morning, but I haven't gotten through to either of them yet.

A. 伝言を頼む B. 返事をもらう C. 用件を伝える D. 電話がつながる

17. Shall we get together on Saturday night and go for a drink or something?

A. 会う B. 買い物する C. 外出する D. 約束を交わす

18. Knowing Mike, it's understandable that nobody gives any credibility to his story of what happened.

A. 信用する　B. 同情する　C. 理解する　D. 面白がる

19. "Do you mind if I sit here?" "Oh, not at all, please go ahead."

A. どうぞ　B. 前に行って　C. 後にして　D. 遠慮して

20. My boyfriend wanted to foot the bill, but I suggested we go Dutch this time.

A. 派手に使う　B. つけにする　C. 割り勘にする　D. おごる

21. At the party, Jenny got really drunk and went overboard with her screaming and shouting.

A. 気がおかしくなった　B. 悲しい目に遭った　C. 度を越した　D. 意識を失った

22. That's the third time you've had a flat. Maybe you should think about buying a new tire.

A. エンストする　B. パンクする　C. オーバーヒートする　D. バッテリーが上がる

23. The new TV series "Family" sure kicked off with a lot of fanfare, didn't it?

A. 始まった　B. 終了した　C. 批判を浴びた　D. 大人気になった

24. Robert, would you knock it off, please? Honestly, you couldn't carry a tune in a bucket!

A. 出ていく B. やめる C. 聞く D. 落ち着く

25. "Do you think Pat will come to the party?" "I wouldn't bank on it."

A. 賭けをする B. 招待する C. 当てにする D. 気にする

26. I think Alex is really onto something with his new invention.

A. あきらめている B. 感づいている C. 結論が出ている D. 知りたがっている

27. The tickets for the jazz festival are usually sold out within an hour or so.

A. 売り切れる B. 売れ残る C. 売り出される D. 発売中止になる

28. As soon as you've learned the ropes in your new position, we'll start giving you more difficult cases to work on.

A. 認められる B. 限界を知る C. コツを覚える D. 仲間を作る

29. We can go to the movie today or tomorrow. It makes no difference to me.

A. どっちでもいい B. 遠慮するな C. 決めさせてほしい D. まだ決めなくてもいい

30. It makes absolutely no sense to me why you choose to live in such a large house on your own.

A. 確められない　B. 理解できない　C. 不公平だ　D. 不当な扱いだ

31. All the guests were disappointed that you weren't able to show up at the reception.

A. スピーチをする　B. 演出する　C. 現れる　D. 盛り上げる

32. If you take a shortcut on your way back to the dorm, you can save at least 20 minutes.

A. ひと休みする　B. 近道する　C. 車を使う　D. 買い物をする

33. When I was a kid, my mom used to chew me out for staying out too late.

A. 迎えに来る　B. 寝かしつける　C. キスをする　D. しかりつける

34. Can I count on you for a $100 contribution to our charity?

A. 貸し出す　B. 担保に取る　C. 当てにする　D. 請求する

35. The boss told us to cut out the unnecessary steps in our workflow to speed things up.

A. 外注する　B. 分担する　C. 削る　D. 書き出す

36. If you happen to be in the area, feel free to drop by my house. You're always welcome.

A. 電話をする　B. 立ち寄る　C. 宿泊する　D. 見物する

37. What is it you're actually trying to get at? Why don't you just come right out and say it?

A. 言おうとする　B. 手に入れようとする　C. 学ぼうとする　D. 見ようとする

38. It wasn't until I was almost 16 that I finally got over my fear of heights.

A. 陥った　B. 理解した　C. 患った　D. 克服した

39. Can you let me off at the station on your way to work, Mark?

A. 探す　B. 降ろす　C. 拾う　D. 付き添う

40. The classical music concert held at the city hall was excellent. It sure lived up to people's expectations.

A. 記憶に残った　B. 期待に応えた　C. 要望を検討した　D. 話題をさらった

2 類義表現を a ～ j の中から選びなさい。

1. blow up
2. end up doing
3. get around
4. hit it off
5. hit the spot
6. hold off
7. jump the gun
8. raise the roof

a. eventually have to do
b. delay
c. be extremely noisy
d. meet
e. act prematurely
f. eat in a restaurant
g. move from one place to another
h. be refreshing; make one feel satisfied
i. lose one's temper
j. start a relationship

---

9. get lost
10. give in
11. keep to oneself
12. lag behind
13. slip one's mind
14. stand out
15. take it easy
16. turn up

a. fail to keep pace
b. learn the basics
c. appear; arrive
d. relax
e. be unique; be visible [noticeable]
f. be forgotten
g. go away
h. be of no consequence
i. yield
j. be introverted

17. bury the hatchet
18. catch on
19. hit the books
20. make waves
21. pull one's leg
22. push one's luck
23. split the bill
24. stay up

a. be useful	b. divide the cost
c. remain awake	d. take a shorter route
e. agree to stop fighting	f. joke; tease
g. go too far; tempt fate	h. become popular
i. cause minor conflicts	j. study

---

25. chip in ～
26. come down with ～
27. figure out ～
28. go over ～
29. keep clear of ～
30. sort out ～
31. stand up for ～
32. wrap up ～

a. resolve	b. anglíry repremand [chastise]
c. contribute	d. catch〈an illness〉
e. defend	f. remove
g. review	h. understand
i. complete	j. avoid

33. call off ～
34. come up with ～
35. cut down on ～
36. give ～ a hand
37. kick around ～
38. put off ～
39. put up with ～
40. turn down ～

a. reject	b. discuss
c. find	d. tolerate; endure
e. reduce	f. imply
g. begin	h. cancel
i. help	j. delay; postpone

復習テスト（Day 1-5）　正解・訳例

1

1. B	2. B	3. C	4. A	5. D	6. A	7. C	8. C	9. C	10. A
11. B	12. B	13. C	14. C	15. D	16. D	17. A	18. A	19. A	20. C
21. C	22. B	23. A	24. B	25. C	26. B	27. A	28. C	29. A	30. B
31. C	32. B	33. D	34. C	35. C	36. B	37. A	38. D	39. B	40. B

1. 「グレアム教授、論文のトピックを変更してもよろしいでしょうか」「ええ、それはまったくあなた次第よ」
2. 学校から家に帰る途中、へんぴな場所で車が故障した。
3. 入学審査委員会は、真夜中過ぎにようやく終わった。
4. 「先週に引っ越した新しいアパートはどう？」「うーん、まあまあってとこかな」
5. パーティーで、最初に私の目に留まったのはアビーだった。
6. ケニーはうわさをまき散らしてばかりで、いつでも騒ぎを起こす羽目になる。
7. みじめな気分のとき、私は山に登るとたいてい元気が出る。
8. コートを持っていったら？　雨が降ったら役立つわ。
9. 「ジムで定期的にトレーニングを始めたって聞いたよ。どんな具合だい？」「最高だよ、リック！」
10. その建築業者は、ダウンタウンの新しい超高層ビル建設で手抜きしたことで、手厳しく非難された。
11. 私は奨学金でやりくりしているのだから、毎日外食するのは金銭的に賢いやり方とはいえない。
12. われわれの競争相手は、コンピューター工学の分野で後れを取っている。
13. 主賓が出席できないと言ったので、パーティーはお流れになった。
14. スーはかなり頭が切れるかもしれないが、付き合いづらい女性だ。
15. 3時間も議論したのに、来年の予算設定について、いっこうにらちが明かなかった。
16. けさからキムとエレンに電話しようとしてるんだけど､まだどっちともつながらないんだ。
17. 土曜の夜に集まって、飲みに行くか何かしない？
18. マイクを知っていれば､起きたことについての彼の説明を誰も信用しないのもうなずける。
19. 「ここに座ってもいい？」「ああ、もちろんだよ。さあどうぞ」
20. ボーイフレンドは勘定を持ちたがったんだけど､今回は割り勘にしようって私が言ったの。
21. パーティーで、ジェニーはすっかり酔っ払い、わめいたり叫んだりが度を越していた。
22. パンクはそれで3度目だ。新しいタイヤを買うことを考えるべきじゃないかな。
23. 新しいテレビ番組の『ファミリー』って、鳴り物入りで始まったよね？

24. ロバート、お願いだからやめてくれないか？　正直に言うと、君はひどい音痴なのかもしれない。
25. 「パットはパーティーに来ると思う？」「当てにはならないと思うよ」
26. アレックスは、自分の新しい発明について、何かピンときていると思うよ。
27. そのジャズフェスティバルのチケットは、たいてい１時間かそこらで売り切れになる。
28. 君が新しいポジションで要領を覚え次第、もっと難しい課題を与え始めるよ。
29. 映画に行くのは今日でも明日でもいい。私はどっちでもかまわないよ。
30. 君がなぜ一人であんなに大きな家に住みたいのか、私にはまったく理解できない。
31. 君がレセプションに出席できなくて、客は皆がっかりしたよ。
32. 寮に戻る途中で近道すれば、少なくとも20分は節約できるよ。
33. 子どものころ、あまり遅くまで出歩いていると、母にこっぴどくしかられたものだった。
34. 私たちの慈善事業に、あなたから100ドルの寄付を当てにしてもいいかしら？
35. 上司は、物事のスピードアップを図るため、私たちに仕事の流れの中で不必要な手順を削るよう命じた。
36. その辺りに来ることがあったら、遠慮なく私の家に立ち寄ってちょうだい。いつでも歓迎するわ。
37. 本当のところ、あなたは何が言いたいのかしら？　単刀直入に言ったらどう？
38. 私は16歳近くになって、ようやく高所恐怖症を克服した。
39. 仕事に行く途中、私を駅で降ろしてくれる、マーク？
40. シティホールで開かれたクラシック音楽のコンサートは秀逸だった。間違いなく人々の期待に応えるものだった。

2

1. i	2. a	3. g	4. j	5. h	6. b	7. e	8. c	9. g	10. i
11. j	12. a	13. f	14. e	15. d	16. c	17. e	18. h	19. j	20. i
21. f	22. g	23. b	24. c	25. c	26. d	27. h	28. g	29. j	30. a
31. e	32. i	33. h	34. c	35. e	36. i	37. b	38. j	39. d	40. a

CD-A6

□ 081 **count out ～**	**～を除外する**、～を外す ≒ not include ～
□ 082 **drop off ～**	**～**〈人・荷物〉**を**〈乗り物から〉**降ろす** ≒ stop to deliver ～
□ 083 **get ahold of ～**	〈電話で〉**～と連絡を取る** ≒ make contact with ～
□ 084 **give ～ a lift**	**～を車に乗せる** ≒ give ～ a ride
□ 085 **go easy on ～**	**～を大目に見る** ≒ not be cruel to ～
□ 086 **let on that ～**	**～を白状する**、～をほのめかす ≒ reveal that ～
□ 087 **look after ～**	**～の面倒を見る**、～を世話する ≒ care for ～; take care of ～
□ 088 **meet ～ halfway**	**～と妥協する** ≒ compromise; find a middle ground

continued ▼

If you're looking for someone to help you cheat on the final exam, count me out.

もし君が期末試験でカンニングの手助けをする人を探しているのなら、私は除外しておいて。

I know it's out of your way, but I need to drop this dry cleaning off on the way home.

あなたの帰り道から外れているのは知っているが、僕は、帰りにこれをドライクリーニングに出さないと駄目なんだ。

Have you been able to get ahold of the tax office? Their lines always seem to be busy when I call.

税務署に電話で連絡が取れたことがあるかい？　私がかけるときはいつも話し中のようだ。

Do you think you could give me a lift to the post office? I don't think I can carry all these packages at the same time.

郵便局まで車に乗せてもらえませんか。私が一度でこれらの荷物をすべて運べるとは思えないんです。

I'd go easy on Ralph. He's a nice person; he just lacks common sense.

ラルフを大目に見るつもりだ。彼はいいやつなんだ、単に常識が欠けているだけさ。

Don't let on that I was the one who told you that rumor.

そのうわさを君に話したのが私だってこと、バラさないで。

If you don't mind, I'd like to ask you to look after my plants while I'm abroad.

もし構わなければ、私が海外に行っている間、植木の面倒を見てもらいたいのですが。

If you are both willing to meet each other halfway, I'm sure you can work out a mutually acceptable solution to the problem.

もしお互いが歩み寄るのをいとわないのであれば、その問題に対して相互に許容できる解決策を打ち出せると思うよ。

continued ▼

CD-A6 (continued)

□ 089 **put ～ into effect**	**～を実施する** ≒ officially start
□ 090 **run into ～**	**～に偶然出会う** ≒ meet ～ by accident
□ 091 **run out of ～**	**～を使い果たす**、～を切らす ≒ use up ～ ; have no more ～
□ 092 **run up against ～**	**～に遭遇する**、～に出くわす ≒ encounter; contend with ～
□ 093 **spell out ～**	**～を〈詳細に〉説明する** ≒ make ～ clear
□ 094 **stop by ～**	**～に立ち寄る** ≒ visit ～ briefly
□ 095 **take over ～**	**～を引き継ぐ** ≒ assume responsibility of ～
□ 096 **work on ～**	**～に働き掛ける**、～の説得に努める ≒ try to convince ～

Last week, the city put a strict anti-smoking policy into effect.	先週、市は厳しい反喫煙方針を実行に移した。
If you happen to run into Jackie, would you mind telling her that I'd like to have a word with her?	もしジャッキーに偶然出会うことがあれば、彼女にちょっと話したいことがあると伝えてもらえませんか。
Pam ran out of gas on the freeway and ended up an hour late for work.	パムは高速道路で（車の）ガソリンを切らして、仕事に1時間も遅刻する羽目になった。
If you run up against anything you can't handle, just give me a call.	もし君の手に負えないことに出くわしたら、とにかく電話して。
The delivery dates and method of payment are clearly spelled out in the contract.	配達日、支払い方法は、契約書の中ではっきり説明されている。
I need to stop by Tim's on the way home and pick up the lecture notes I loaned him.	家に帰る途中でティムのところに寄って、彼に貸した講義メモを取ってこなければいけない。
The new dean will take over your duties at the beginning of the next academic year.	新しい学部長は、次の学年度の初めにあなたの職務を引き継ぐだろう。
I think if you continue to work on your father he'll eventually let you move into your own apartment.	お父さんを説得し続ければ、ゆくゆくはあなたをアパートに引っ越させてくれると思うよ。

CD-A7

□ 097 **take advantage of ～**	**～を利用する** ≒ make good use of ～; use ～ to one's advantage
□ 098 **take care of ～**	**～の面倒を見る** ≒ look after ～
□ 099 **trade in ～**	**～を下取りに出す** ≒ exchange; replace
□ 100 **turn in ～**	**～を提出する** ≒ submit
□ 101 **work out ～**	**～を解決する**、〈自動詞で〉解決する、うまくいく ≒ solve; be sucessful
□ 102 **down the drain**	**無駄になって**、浪費されて ≒ wasted
□ 103 **in the dark**	**知らずに**、わからずに ≒ unaware
□ 104 **nothing short of ～**	**ほとんど～で**、～同然の ≒～ at the very least

continued ▼

Students at our university can take advantage of its extensive science library — the biggest in the country!

当大学の学生は、広大な科学図書館を利用できます――この国で一番大きいんです！

Do you intend to take care of your parents when they get older?

両親が年老いたら、面倒を見るつもりですか。

I need to trade in my unreliable old car for a newer one.

頼りにならない中古車を下取りに出して、もっと新しい車を買わなければ。

The one thing Professor Johnson insists on is that all homework be turned in on time.

ジョンソン教授が強く求める唯一のことは、すべての宿題を期限通りに提出するというものである。

You two need to work out the problems with your project before the end of the semester.

君たち２人は、学期が終わる前に、手掛けているプロジェクトの例の問題点を解決する必要がある。

If you're not careful, all your efforts will go right down the drain.

注意しないとすべての努力が無駄になるだろう。

Vera is totally in the dark about why you haven't called her recently.

ベラは、近ごろなぜあなたが電話をしてくれなかったのか、まったくわからずにいる。

Dennis's speedy recovery from his knee operation was nothing short of amazing.

デニスのひざの手術からの早い回復は、まったく驚くに値するものだった。

continued ▼

CD-A7(continued)

□ 105 **all at once**	**突然に** ≒ suddenly
□ 106 **for a change**	**気分転換に**、たまには ≒ instead of doing the usual thing
□ 107 **in a flash**	**直ちに**、あっという間に ≒ very soon
□ 108 **in a nutshell**	**手短に**、簡潔に ≒ briefly
□ 109 **no way**	**決して〜ない**、決して〜できない •no wayの前にthere isを補ってもよい。 ≒ not a chance
□ 110 **on and off**	**断続的に**、時々 ≒ periodically
□ 111 **on short notice**	**急に**、即座に ≒ with little preparation time
□ 112 (every) **once in a while**	**時々** ≒ occasionally

All at once, I realized that my impression of Lynn had been wrong all of these years.

突然、私のリンに対する長年の印象が間違っていたことを悟った。

How about spending Saturday afternoon at the beach for a change?

たまには土曜日の午後、海岸で過ごすのはどう？

I'll be back in a flash. I just need to run to the bank for a few minutes.

すぐに戻ってくるよ。銀行に数分で走って行ってくるだけだ。

Just tell me what happened in a nutshell; I don't have time for the whole story.

何があったのか手短に教えて。全部を聞く時間はないから。

There is no way I'd consider swimming in such a polluted river!

こんなに汚染された川で泳ぐことなんて、絶対に考えられないよ！

I listen to jazz on and off, whenever the spirit moves me.

私は時々ジャズを聞いているんだ、いつでも気の向いた時にね。

This new assignment is due tomorrow! I can't do it on such short notice.

この新しい課題は明日が締め切りだって！そんなに急にはできないよ。

I know it's not healthy, but once in a while I really get the urge to eat a big, juicy steak.

健康的ではないとわかっているが、時々大きくて肉汁たっぷりのステーキを食べたい衝動に駆られる。

CD-A8

□ 113 **for nothing**	**無駄に**、無駄な ≒ in vain
□ 114 **from scratch**	**最初から**、ゼロから ≒ from the very beginning
□ 115 **in nothing flat**	**直ちに**、すぐに ≒ very quickly
□ 116 (every) **now and then**	**時々** ≒ once in a while
□ 117 **on cloud nine**	**うきうきして** ≒ feeling extremely happy
□ 118 **over and over**	**何度も何度も** ≒ repeatedly
□ 119 **through the grapevine**	**人づてに**、人のうわさで ≒ as a rumor
□ 120 **you bet**	**確かに**、間違いなく ≒ absolutely; for sure

continued ▼

Jim claims that it wasn't for nothing that he decided to work for a few years before entering college.

ジムは、大学に入る前に数年間働くと決断したことは無駄ではなかった、と主張している。

I accidentally erased the file I was working on. Now I'll have to start over from scratch.

取り組んでいたファイルをうっかり消してしまった。また最初からやり直さなければならない。

If you're hungry, I can make you an omelet in nothing flat.

もしおなかがすいているなら、すぐにオムレツを作ってあげられるよ。

Now that your e-mail is working again, make sure that you send me a message now and then.

君のＥメールはまた正常に動作するようになっているのだから、時々私にメッセージを送るようにしてください。

I've been on cloud nine ever since I found out my paper was accepted for publication.

自分の論文が出版の運びとなったことに気付いて、私はうきうきしている。

I've told you over and over that you need to fasten your seat belt if you ride with me.

私と一緒に車に乗るときはシートベルトを締めて、と何度も何度もあなたに言いましたよ。

I heard through the grapevine that you're thinking of studying abroad in your junior year. Is it true?

大学３年生になったら海外留学しようと考えているって人づてに聞いたよ。それは本当？

Am I excited about going to Disneyland? You bet I am!

ディズニーランドへ行くのにわくわくしてるかって？　もちろんそうさ！

continued ▼

CD-A8(continued)

□ 121 **a good sport**	**さっぱりした人**、気さくな人、いい人 ≒ an easygoing person
□ 122 **no big deal**	**大したことではない**、重要でない ≒ not an important issue
□ 123 **pros and cons**	**賛否**(の意見)、善し悪し ≒ advantages and disadvantages
□ 124 **the green light**	**許可**、お墨付き ≒ approval; official sanction
□ 125 **the last straw**	**我慢の限界** ≒ the limit; all I can take
□ 126 (the) **chances are** (that) ～	**たぶん～だろう** ≒ it is likely (that) ～
□ 127 **Not again!**	**またかよ！**、またなの！ ≒ Oh no! Yet another time!
□ 128 **Search me.**	**わからない。**、知らない。 ≒ I have no idea.

You sure are a good sport, Alice. Making those extra copies was way beyond your job description.	君は本当にいい人だね、アリス。余分なコピーを取るのは、君の契約した仕事内容をはるかに超えていたのに。
We're not so busy today; it's no big deal if you decide to take the rest of the day off.	今日はあまり忙しくない。君がこの日の残りを休むことにしてもどうってことないよ。
You don't need to make up your mind this instant. All I ask is that you listen to the pros and cons before deciding.	今この時点で決める必要はない。私が求めているのは、決定する前に君が賛否両論を聞くことだけだ。
The reason I haven't started my term paper is that I'm waiting for Professor Sellen to give my topic the green light.	私が期末リポートに取り掛かっていないのは、セレン教授が私の題材にお墨付きをくれるのを待っているからだ。
That's the last straw, Mike. You're fired!	我慢の限界だ、マイク。君は首だ！
John is late for work. Chances are that he's stuck in traffic again.	ジョンは会社に遅れている。たぶんまた渋滞につかまっているんだろう。
Not again! That's the fourth time this week. Won't you ever learn?	またかよ！　今週４回目だ。いつになったらわかるんだい？
Search me. I haven't got a clue what Ted's thinking, either.	さあね。テッドが何を考えているのか、僕にもさっぱりわからない。

CD-A9

□ 129 **bark up the wrong tree**	**見当違いなことをする**、お門違いな非難をする ≒ look in the wrong place
□ 130 **be booked up**	**予約でいっぱいである** ≒ have no time available
□ 131 **bend over backwards**	**全力を尽くす**、骨を折る ≒ do more than one usually would
□ 132 **bring home the bacon**	**生活の糧を稼ぐ** ≒ support the family
□ 133 **call it a day**	〈仕事などを〉**切り上げる**、終わりにする ≒ finish work for the day
□ 134 **come out smelling like a rose**	〈問題がなかったかのように〉**うまく切り抜ける** ≒ emerge from a bad situation successfully
□ 135 **count your chickens before they're hatched**	**捕らぬたぬきの皮算用をする** ・成功・勝利などを実現しないうちから確実だと思うこと。 ≒ expect the best outcome
□ 136 **die of hunger**	**おなかがペコペコだ** ≒ be very hungry; be starving [famished]

continued ▼

You're barking up the wrong tree if you think Trudy would do something like that.

トルーディーがそんなことをすると思うなら、見当違いだ。

I wanted to visit the dentist tomorrow, but she's booked up until next week.

明日歯医者に行きたかったんだけど、来週まで予約でいっぱいだね。

I keep bending over backwards trying to please my roommate, but she never appreciates anything I do.

ルームメートを満足させようと全力を尽くしているが、彼女は私がすることに決して感謝しない。

Helen doesn't care what her future husband looks like. She just wants someone who can bring home the bacon.

ヘレンは、未来の夫となる人の見た目は気にしない。生活の糧を稼ぐことができる人をただ望んでいるんだ。

Paul, you've been working on the computer since early morning. Why don't you call it a day?

ポール、君は早朝からパソコン作業に取り組んでいるね。切り上げたらどう？

Norm forgot his lecture notes, but he's such a good speaker that he came out smelling like a rose.

ノームは講義メモを忘れたが、話が非常に上手なのでそんなことがなかったかのようにうまく切り抜けた。

You don't know you'll get the job for sure, so don't count your chickens before they're hatched.

確実にその仕事に就けるかどうかわからないんだから、捕らぬたぬきの皮算用をするな。

Can you hurry up with dinner? I'm dying of hunger right now.

晩ごはんを急いでくれるかな？　ちょうど今、おなかがペコペコなんだ。

continued
▼

CD-A9 (continued)

□ 137 **eat like a horse**	**よく食べる**、大食いする ≒ eat a lot
□ 138 **fill A in on B**	**A**(人)**に B**(物事)**について詳しく説明する** ≒ inform A of B
□ 139 **get into the swing of things**	**調子が出る** ≒ get used to the situation
□ 140 **get it over with**	**けりをつける**、決着をつける ≒ finish it
□ 141 **get on the ball**	**気を引き締める** ≒ organize oneself
□ 142 **have a chip on one's shoulder**	**けんか腰である**、怒りっぽい ≒ have a bad attitude
□ 143 **have it coming**	**自業自得である** ≒ deserve it
□ 144 **snap out of it**	**元気を出す**、気を取り直す ≒ wake up; get over it

Your baby boy seems healthy: he's eating like a horse every time I see him.

あなたの坊やは健康そうだね。見るたびによく食べているし。

Could you fill me in on what I missed while I was away on vacation?

私が休暇でいなかった間に聞けなかったことについて、詳しく説明していただけませんか。

All new students are confused at first. After you get into the swing of things, everything will come much easier.

すべての新入生が初めは戸惑うんだ。調子が出てきたら、すべてのことがずっと楽になるだろう。

When you can't escape doing something unpleasant, the best thing to do is simply to get it over with as soon as possible.

気が向かないことをやらなければならないとき、一番良い方法は単にできるだけ早くけりをつけることだ。

I'd get on the ball, if I were you, Karen. You're in danger of failing this class.

もし君の立場だったら僕は気を引き締めるよ、カレン。だって君はこのクラスで落第の危機にあるんだから。

Brian has had a real chip on his shoulder ever since his girlfriend left him.

ブライアンはガールフレンドに振られてからずっと、本当にけんか腰だ。

If you fail math because of not handing in any assignments, you can't say you didn't have it coming.

宿題をまったく提出しなかったせいで数学で落第しても、それは自業自得だ。

I hope Joanne snaps out of it soon. It's been six months since her dog died and she's got to get on with her life.

ジョアンには早く元気を出してほしい。彼女の飼っていた犬は亡くなって6カ月たつのだから、前向きに生きていかなくては。

CD-A10

□ 145
be back on one's feet

回復する
≒ recover completely

□ 146
fly off the handle

かっとなる
≒ become suddenly angry

□ 147
get off the phone

電話を切る
≒ finish talking on the phone

□ 148
go back to square one

振り出しに戻る
≒ begin over; go back to the beginning

□ 149
go in one ear and out the other

(右から左に)**聞き流される**
≒ be not listened to

□ 150
have a heart of gold

優しい、思いやりがある
≒ be very kind

□ 151
keep one's nose to the grindstone

あくせく働く、～をこき使う
≒ keep working hard

□ 152
keep track of ～

～の経過をたどる、～の消息[動向]をつかむ
≒ maintain a record of ～

continued ▼

I heard your accident was pretty serious. When do you expect to be back on your feet?	君が遭った事故はかなり深刻だったと聞きました。いつごろ回復しそうですか。
Bob flies off the handle at the slightest provocation.	ボブはちょっとした挑発でかっとなる。
Could you please get off the phone, Jerry? I need to call my mother to wish her a happy birthday.	電話を切ってくれるかな、ジェリー？母に誕生日のお祝いの電話をしなくてはいけないんだ。
Since the experiment failed, we'll have to go right back to square one and start all over again.	実験は失敗したのだから、全くの振り出しに戻って、また最初からやり直さなければならない。
Anything you tell Brad goes in one ear and out the other.	あなたがブラッドに言うことはすべて、聞き流されている。
Your grandmother has a heart of gold; it was so kind of her to bake me those cookies.	君のおばあさんは優しいね。僕のためにクッキーを焼いてくれるなんてとても親切だった。
If you keep your nose to the grindstone every day, you'll be amazed at how much you can accomplish.	毎日あくせくして働いたら、どれだけのことが成し遂げられるかに驚くだろう。
So many new classes are being offered that I can't keep track of all the recent changes in the course catalog.	非常にたくさんの新しい授業が提供されているので、コースカタログで最近の変化の動向のすべてはつかむことができない。

continued
▼

CD-A10(continued)

□ 153 **leave A up to B**	**A(物事)をB(人)に任せる** ≒ rely upon B to do A
□ 154 **let up**	**仕事の手を休める** ≒ stop working hard
□ 155 **lose the thread**	**話の筋がわからなくなる** ≒ move away from the main point
□ 156 **make A out to be B**	(事実に反して)**AをBであると主張する** ≒ describe A as B; imagine A to be B
□ 157 **make ends meet**	**収入内で暮らす**、帳尻を合わせる ≒ pay one's expenses
□ 158 **roll up one's sleeves**	**仕事に取り掛かる**、腕まくりをする ≒ get to work
□ 159 **sink in**	**十分に理解される**、身に染みる ≒ feel real; become clear
□ 160 **stick one's neck out**	**自ら身を危険にさらす** ≒ take a risk

The thing I like about that travel agency is that I can leave everything up to them; I don't have to worry about a thing.	その旅行業者の良いところは、全部を任せられるところだ。何も心配する必要がないんだ。
Why don't you let up for a while and take a break?	しばらくの間仕事の手を休めて休暇を取ったらどう？
Ike's talk was really disjointed; he kept losing the thread of what he wanted to say.	アイクの話は本当に支離滅裂だった。彼は、言いたかったことから話の筋がそれてばかりだったんだ。
You shouldn't make me out to be a saint; I'm just a normal person like you.	私を聖者のように思うべきではありませんよ。ただ、あなたのような普通の人間にすぎないのだから。
I have no idea how I'm going to make ends meet now that my application for financial aid has been turned down.	学費援助の申し込みが却下された今、どうやって収入内で暮らしていったらいいのかわからない。
Let's roll up our sleeves and get this project finished.	腕まくりをして取り掛かって、このプロジェクトを終わらせよう。
It hasn't completely sunk in yet that I was elected class president.	僕が学級委員長に選ばれたなんて、まだあまり実感がわかない。
Thanks for sticking your neck out for me; you really didn't have to do that.	私のために危険に身をさらしてくれてありがとう。本当はそうする義務などなかったのに。

復習テスト (Day 6-10)

(正解・訳例は pp.78-79)

1 赤字の意味としてもっともふさわしいものを A ～ D の中から選びなさい。

1. Say, Patti, where are you going? I can give you a lift if you want.

A. 手を貸す　B. 案内する　C. お願いをする　D. 車に乗せる

2. Jack didn't let on that he was thinking about changing his major.

A. 気にする　B. 白状する　C. 隠す　D. 相談する

3. Cheryl was helping her friend look after the flower shop.

A. 見て回る　B. 買い物する　C. 卸す　D. 面倒を見る

4. In order to solve the problem, you will have to meet him halfway in the end.

A. 除外する　B. 理解する　C. 妥協する　D. 協力する

5. The police put a curfew into effect for the city.

A. 強要する　B. 許可する　C. 検討する　D. 実施する

6. I hadn't seen my uncle in almost 10 years when I ran into him at the mall.

A. ばったり出会った　B. 話し合った　C. 電話した　D. うわさを聞いた

7. When Professor Freedman talked about cheating, he spelled out the consequences pretty clearly.

A. 詳しく説明した　B. 予測した　C. つづりを略して書いた　D. 外部に漏らした

8. Can I stop by your place later? I've got something I need to talk to you about.

A. 泊まりに行く　B. ちょっと寄る　C. メールする　D. 迎えに行く

9. There's a textbook sale at the bookshop right now, so I'm going to go take advantage of it.

A. 調査する　B. 利用する　C. 比較する　D. 応援する

10. "Are you free this afternoon, Jim?" "No, actually I've got something important to take care of."

A. 気分を晴らす　B. 気を紛らわせる　C. 手の内を明かす　D. 面倒を見る

11. I need to trade in this old computer; it's too slow.

A. 修理してもらう　B. 改造する　C. 下取りに出す　D. 海外に輸出する

12. Terry got a notice from the library because he forgot to turn in the books he borrowed.

A. 整理する　B. 弁償する　C. 登録する　D. 返却する

13. Jane and Lydia need to work out their personal issues outside of the classroom.

A. 分析する　B. 解決する　C. 運動する　D. 議論する

14. Jake's proposal to change this old-fashioned system is nothing short of brilliant.

A. まったく現実的ではない　B. かなりあいまいだ　C. 絶対にいい考えだ　D. まったく見当違いだ

15. "Can you give me a hand with this, Yoko?" "Sure, wait! I'll be back in a flash."

A. すぐに　B. しばらくして　C. ひと休みした後　D. 身支度をして

16. Once in a while, Martha and I get together to go drinking and chasing guys.

A. 時折　B. 長年　C. 近ごろ　D. いつの間にか

17. Kevin sure is a good sport to take all the teasing you give him about his weight without getting upset.

A. スポーツマン　B. いい人　C. 打たれ強い人　D. 恥ずかしがり屋

18. "I heard Barry got straight A's this term." "It's no big deal. He does that every term."

A. 大したことではない　B. まぐれではない　C. めったにないことだ　D. 大変珍しいことだ

19. In debate, you need to look at both the pros and cons of a matter.

A. さまざまな要素　B. 原因と結果　C. 良い面と悪い面　D. プロとアマチュア

20. The committee members have given the green light to the new campus development project.

A. 助言した　B. 援助した　C. 批判した　D. 許可した

21. "Jack's had another accident." "That's the last straw; I'm not going to let him use my car ever again!"

A. 注意不足　B. 期待外れ　C. 我慢の限界　D. 毎度のこと

22. You can try calling her but chances are that she's already on the plane.

A. おそらく　B. 絶対に　C. 運よく　D. 困ったことに

23. "I dozed off right in the middle of the literature class." "Not again!"

A. それ以上言わないで　B. またなの　C. 知らなかったわ　D. 初めてだね

24. "Do you know why they couldn't make it on time?" "Search me!"

A. もちろん　B. 当ててごらん　C. わからない　D. 内緒だよ

25. Alice has nothing to do with this problem, John; you're barking up the wrong tree.

A. 見当違いなことをしている　B. 間違いを認めている　C. 非難が度を越している　D. 深入りし過ぎている

26. The restaurant is booked up until 9 p.m; is that too late?

A. 入店制限がある　B. 営業中である　C. 貸し切りになっている　D. 予約でいっぱいだ

27. You look tired, Mason. Let's call it a day and we'll finish this off tomorrow.

A. 打ち合わせる　B. 日報を書く　C. 切り上げる　D. ちょっと休憩する

28. Junko overslept and was late for her job interview, but she still came out smelling like a rose. I guess they really wanted her for that job.

A. 何でもないふりをした　B. うまく切り抜けた　C. 落ち込んでいた　D. 顔が硬直していた

29. "I heard a rumor that I might be promoted to vice president, so I decided to buy a new car." "I think you're counting your chickens before they're hatched."

A. 一石二鳥　B. あぶはち取らず　C. 猫に小判　D. 捕らぬたぬきの皮算用

30. We can eat out now, or cook at home later. What do you think? Are you really dying of hunger?

A. おなかがペコペコだ　B. 胃の調子が悪い　C. 満腹感でいっぱいだ　D. ダイエット中だ

31. I usually eat like a horse, but I never seem to gain any weight.

A. 大食いする　B. 菜食主義である　C. 小食である　D. 早食いする

32. Satoshi, how was Professor Brett's lecture? Can you fill me in on what he talked about?

A. 説明する　B. 評価する　C. 書き込む　D. 説得する

33. My mother irritates me a lot. She always tells me to get off the phone while I'm still talking to someone.

A. 電話に出る　B. 電話を代わる　C. 電話番号を伝える　D. 電話を切る

34. The deal with the computer company fell through, so we need to go back to square one.

A. 借金を返済する　B. 身動きが取れなくなる　C. 本部に持ち帰る　D. 振り出しに戻る

35. My father-in-law never takes what I say seriously. It just goes in one ear and out the other.

A. 右から左に聞き流される　B. 違ったとらえ方をされる　C. 聞くのを拒まれる　D. 聞いていないふりをされる

36. Dr. Joshua's students really have to keep their noses to the grindstone in her class, don't they?

A. 一生懸命勉強する　B. 鼻っ柱をへし折られる　C. 常に意見を述べる　D. 経済的に自立する

37. Mike has had so many different types of job that it's almost impossible to keep track of them all.

A. 数える B. 日記をつける C. 忘れ去る D. 跡をたどる

38. Don't worry about doing any cleaning. Just leave everything up to me.

A. 私にすべて振り分けさせて B. 私にすべてを任せて C. 私の分もすべて取っておいて D. 私にすべてやらせないで

39. I was so upset while we were talking that I completely lost the thread of our conversation.

A. 話の筋がわからなくなった B. 話をめちゃくちゃにした
C. 話を切り上げた D. 話の途中で割り込んだ

40. The food in the cafeteria is not always as bad as it's made out to be.

A. 思われている B. 作られている C. 販売されている D. 処分されている

2 類義表現を a ～ j の中から選びなさい。

1. count out ～
2. drop off ～
3. get ahold of ～
4. go easy on ～
5. run out of ～
6. run up against ～
7. take over ～
8. work on ～

a. try to convince ～
b. use up ～; have no more ～
c. make contact with ～
d. rely on ～; depend on ～
e. recover from ～
f. do not include ～
g. encounter; contend with ～
h. assume responsibility of ～
i. stop to deliver ～
j. do not be cruel to ～

---

9. down the drain
10. in the dark
11. all at once
12. for a change
13. in a nutshell
14. no way
15. on and off
16. on short notice

a. very soon
b. not a chance
c. briefly
d. not an important issue
e. with little preparation time
f. instead of doing the usual thing
g. periodically
h. unaware
i. wasted
j. suddenly

17. for nothing
18. from scratch
19. in nothing flat
20. (every) now and then
21. on cloud nine
22. over and over
23. through the grapevine
24. you bet

a. every day
b. once in a while
c. in vain
d. as a rumor
e. more than that
f. absolutely; for sure
g. very quickly
h. from the very beginning
i. repeatedly
j. feeling extremely happy

---

25. bend over backwards
26. bring home the bacon
27. get into the swing of things
28. get it over with
29. get on the ball
30. have a chip on one's shoulder
31. have it coming
32. snap out of it

a. finish it
b. do more than one usually would
c. wake up; get over it
d. get used to the situation
e. deserve it
f. eat a lot
g. have a bad attitude
h. move away from the main point
i. support the family
j. organize oneself

33. be back on one's feet
34. fly off the handle
35. have a heart of gold
36. let up
37. make ends meet
38. roll up one's sleeves
39. sink in
40. stick one's neck out

a. get to work
b. feel real; become clear
c. become suddenly angry
d. expect the best outcome
e. take a risk
f. be very kind
g. finish work for the day
h. pay one's expenses
i. stop working hard
j. recover completely

復習テスト（Day 6-10） 正解・訳例

1

1. D	2. B	3. D	4. C	5. D	6. A	7. A	8. B	9. B	10. D
11. C	12. D	13. B	14. C	15. A	16. A	17. B	18. A	19. C	20. D
21. C	22. A	23. B	24. C	25. A	26. D	27. C	28. B	29. D	30. A
31. A	32. A	33. D	34. D	35. A	36. A	37. D	38. B	39. A	40. A

1. ねえ、パティ、どこに行くの？ よかったら、車で送ってあげるよ。
2. 専攻を変えようと考えていることを、ジャックはおくびにも出さなかった。
3. シェリルは、友達が花屋の管理をするのを手伝っていた。
4. 問題解決のために、君は結局は彼と妥協しなくてはならないだろう。
5. 警察は、その都市に対して夜間外出禁止令を実施した。
6. 私は、ショッピングセンターでばったり出会うまで、おじにほぼ10年会っていなかった。
7. フリードマン教授は、カンニングについて話した時、その結果どうなるかをかなり明確に説明した。
8. 後で君の家に寄ってもいいかな？ 君に話さなきゃならないことがあるんだ。
9. ちょうど今、本屋で教科書の安売りをやっているので、私はそれを利用しに行くつもりだ。
10. 「今日の午後は暇なの、ジム？」「いや、実はやらなきゃならない大事な用があるんだ」
11. この古いコンピューターは下取りに出さないと。（反応が）遅過ぎるんだ。
12. テリーは、借りた本の返却を忘れたので、図書館から通知をもらった。
13. ジェーンとリディアは、自らの個人的な問題について教室の外で解決する必要がある。
14. この旧式のシステムを変更するというジェイクの提案は、素晴らしいと言うほかない。
15. 「これ手伝ってくれる、ヨウコ？」「もちろん、ちょっと待ってて！ すぐ戻るから」
16. 時々、マーサと私は一緒に飲みに行って、男性に言い寄ったりしてるの。
17. 体重のことで君があれだけからかっても怒らず受け流すんだから、ケビンって本当に気のいいやつだよな。
18. 「バリーは今学期オールAだったって聞いたわ」「大騒ぎすることじゃないさ。彼は毎学期そうだもの」
19. ディベートでは、物事の良い面と悪い面の両方を見る必要がある。
20. 委員会のメンバーたちは、新キャンパス開発プロジェクトにお墨付きを与えた。
21. 「ジャックがまた事故を起こしたの」「もう我慢の限界だ。二度と私の車は使わせないぞ！」
22. 彼女に電話してみてもいいが、彼女はおそらくもう飛行機に乗っているだろう。
23. 「文学の授業の真っ最中に居眠りしちゃった」「またなの！」
24. 「彼らが間に合わなかった訳、知ってる？」「知らないよ！」

25. ジョン、アリスはこの問題とは無関係だ。君の非難はお門違いだよ。
26. レストランは午後9時まで予約がいっぱいよ。それじゃ遅過ぎない？
27. 疲れてるみたいね、メーソン。今日はもう切り上げて、これは明日仕上げましょう。
28. ジュンコったら、寝過ごして仕事の面接に遅れたのに、うまく切り抜けたのよ。相手方は、あの仕事にどうしても彼女が欲しかったようね。
29. 「僕が副社長に昇進するかもしれないってうわさを聞いたんで、新しい車を買うことにしたよ」「それは、捕らぬたぬきの皮算用じゃないかしら」
30. 今外食してもいいし、後から家で料理してもいい。どう？　本当に死にそうなほどおなかがペコペコなの？
31. 僕はいつも大食いなんだけど、全然太らないみたいなんだ。
32. サトシ、ブレット教授の講義はどうだった？　僕に教授の話の内容を詳しく説明してくれるかい？
33. 母ったら本当にうっとうしいの。いつでも、私がまだ話し中なのに、その電話を切れって言うのよ。
34. そのコンピューター会社との取引はご破算になったので、私たちは振り出しに戻る必要がある。
35. 義理の父は、私の言うことを真剣に取らない。ただ聞き流されてしまうんだ。
36. ジョシュア教授のところの学生って、クラスで本当にあくせく勉強しなくちゃならないんですってね？
37. マイクは実に多くの、さまざまな種類の仕事をしてきたので、その経過をすべてたどることはほとんど不可能だ。
38. 掃除のことは気にしないで。すべて、私にただ任せてちょうだい。
39. 話していた時、私はあまりにも取り乱していたので、話の筋がすっかりわからなくなった。
40. カフェテリアの食べ物は、言われているほどいつもまずいというわけではない。

2

1. f	2. i	3. c	4. j	5. b	6. g	7. h	8. a	9. i	10. h
11. j	12. f	13. c	14. b	15. g	16. e	17. c	18. h	19. g	20. b
21. j	22. i	23. d	24. f	25. b	26. i	27. d	28. a	29. j	30. g
31. e	32. c	33. j	34. c	35. f	36. i	37. h	38. a	39. b	40. e

CD-A11

□ 161 **beat around the bush**	**遠回しに言う** ≒ talk indirectly
□ 162 **cost ～ an arm and a leg**	**～にとって多額の出費になる** ≒ be very expensive
□ 163 **drop in on ～**	**～をひょいと訪れる**、～にちょっと立ち寄る ≒ visit ～ briefly
□ 164 **fall on hard times**	**つらい目に遭う**、落ちぶれる ≒ encounter financial difficulties
□ 165 **get around to doing**	**～に手が回る**、～する〈時間的〉余裕を見つける ≒ find time to do
□ 166 **grab a bite**	**軽く食事をする** ≒ quickly get something to eat
□ 167 **have a way with words**	**話し上手である** ≒ use language skillfully
□ 168 **have other fish to fry**	**ほかに大事な用事[やるべきこと]がある** ≒ have other interests

continued ▼

Stop beating around the bush and get to the point.

遠回しに言うのをやめて、はっきり言ってよ。

That's a gorgeous overcoat, Peter. It must have cost you an arm and a leg.

それは豪華なコートだね、ピーター。きっと高かったんだろうね。

You don't need to phone first; drop in on me anytime.

あらかじめ電話をする必要はないよ。いつでも立ち寄って。

In this economy, it's not surprising that many small companies have fallen on hard times.

この景気では、多くの零細企業がつらい目に遭ったのも無理はない。

Did you ever get around to cleaning out your garage?

ガレージの掃除にまで手が回りましたか。

If you're hungry, we could grab a bite at that burger shop down the road.

おなかがすいているなら、その道を下ったところにあるあのハンバーガーショップで軽く食事を取ることもできますよ。

Jerry surely has a way with words; he's very persuasive.

ジェリーは本当に話し上手だ。とても説得力がある。

Probably the reason Joe isn't participating in the concert is because he has other fish to fry.

おそらくジョーがコンサートに参加していない理由は、ほかに大事な用事があるからだ。

continued ▼

CD-A11 (continued)

□169 **knock oneself out**	**全力を尽くす**、一生懸命やる ≒ work too hard
□170 **lose one's train of thought**	**言おうとしたことを忘れる** ≒ forget what one planned to say
□171 **not miss a beat**	**とまどわない**、ちゅうちょしない、まごつかない ≒ be really sharp; be on the ball
□172 **pick up the tab**	**勘定を持つ** ≒ pick up the bill; pay for everything

□173 **scratch the surface**	**上面をなでる**、表面的に扱う ≒ fulfill a small amount
□174 **take out A on B**	**A**〈怒りなど〉**を B に**〈八つ当たり的に〉**ぶつける** ≒ misdirect anger about A toward B
□175 **take some time off**	**休暇を取る** ≒ take a break [vacation]
□176 **talk A out of B**	**A を説得して B をやめさせる** ≒ dissuade A from B

You don't need to knock yourself out finishing that report tonight; it's not due until the end of the week.

そのリポートを今夜頑張って終わらせる必要はないよ。締め切りは週末までじゃないから。

Now, what was I saying? I've lost my train of thought.

今、僕は何て言ってたかな？　言おうとしたことを忘れちゃった。

Betty doesn't miss a beat when it comes to remembering people's names.

ベティーは、人の名前を思い出すとなるととまどいがない。

No one can ever accuse Penny of being stingy; every time I've had dinner with her, she's always picked up the tab.

誰もペニーをけちだと非難することはできない。私が彼女と夕食を取るときはいつでも、彼女が勘定を払っているんだから。

Debbie hasn't even scratched the surface of her potential as a chemist.

デビーはまだ化学者としての自分の可能性の一端をかじってさえいない。

Melissa often takes her anger out on other people.

メリッサは、しばしば他人に八つ当たりをする。

You've been working seven days a week for two months now. Don't you think you should take some time off, for a few days at least?

君はもう２カ月もの間、毎日休みなく働き続けているんだ。少なくとも2、３日は休暇を取るべきだと思わない？

I really hope you can talk George out of quitting his job.

ジョージが仕事を辞めないように君が説得できたらって、本当に願っているんだ。

CD-A12

☐ 177
break the ice

場を和ませる、話の口火を切る
≒ create a relaxed atmosphere

☐ 178
go out on a limb

危険を冒す、困難な立場になる
≒ take a risk

☐ 179
have a lot on one's mind

いろいろ考えることがある、頭がいっぱいだ
≒ be preoccupied

☐ 180
have it in for ～

～に敵意を抱いている
≒ dislike and want to harm ～

☐ 181
have it out

議論で片を付ける、徹底的に話し合う
≒ argue frankly

☐ 182
have two strikes against ～

～にとって不利な立場にある
≒ be at a major disadvantage

☐ 183
help oneself to ～

～を自由に取って食べる
≒ take ～ freely; take ～ for oneself

☐ 184
hit the nail on the head

核心を突く、的を射る
≒ be exactly right

continued ▼

Telling a joke is sometimes a good way to break the ice.

冗談を言うことは、場を和ませるのによい方法になることがある。

Don't let me down, Rick. I really went out on a limb for you.

がっかりさせないでよ、リック。君のために本当に危険を冒したんだから。

Don't be so hard on Glen. He's really had a lot on his mind recently.

グレンにつらく当たらないで。彼は最近本当にいろいろ心配事を抱えているんだ。

No matter how hard I try, I can never please my supervisor. I'm convinced she has it in for me.

どんなに私が一生懸命やっても、上司を決して喜ばせることはできない。私は、彼女が私に敵意を抱いていることを確信している。

Dana had it out with her dorm advisor last night, but now she regrets having gotten so angry.

デーナはゆうべ寮のアドバイザーとやり合って決着を付けたが、今彼女はあんなに怒ったことを後悔している。

Considering the fact that she got evicted from her last apartment, I'd say Linda has two strikes against her in trying to find a new place to live.

リンダが前のアパートから立ち退かされたという事実を考えると、新しく住む場所を見つけようとするのに彼女は不利な立場にあると思う。

Help yourself to some coffee; I just made a fresh pot.

コーヒーをご自由にどうぞ。ちょうど新しく入れたところなんだ。

You hit the nail on the head when you said Jake would probably be late for work again today.

ジェークがたぶん今日もまた仕事に遅れてくるだろうと君は言ったけれど、的中したよ。

continued ▼

CD-A12(continued)

□ 185 **keep in touch**	**連絡を取り合う** ≒ maintain contact
□ 186 **keep up with ～**	**～に遅れないようついていく** ≒ maintain the same level with ～
□ 187 **pull off ～**	**～をうまくやってのける** ≒ accomplish
□ 188 **rub ～ the wrong way**	**～の神経を逆なでする** ≒ cause ～ irritation; make ～ annoyed
□ 189 **rub in ～**	**～**〈失敗・欠点〉**をわざと繰り返し言う** ≒ tease someone for ～ they are already embarrased about
□ 190 **see eye to eye**	**意見が合う** ≒ agree
□ 191 **sign up for ～**	**～を**〈署名の上〉**申し込む** ≒ register for ～
□ 192 **turn over a new leaf**	**心を入れ替える**、心機一転する ≒ change one's ways [habits]

Let's make sure that we keep in touch even after you move to Denver.

君がデンバーに引っ越した後でも、連絡を取り合えるようにしておこう。

If you don't keep up with your reading, you'll start falling behind other people in the class.

もし君が読書課題についていかないなら、クラスのほかの人たちから遅れ始めるだろう。

Well, I pulled it off. No one thought I could finish that term paper before the deadline, but I did.

ええと、うまくやったよ。誰も私が締め切り前に期末リポートを終わらせることができるとは思っていなかったけれど、やったんだ。

You know, sometimes my roommate's behavior really rubs me the wrong way.

ところで、時々、ルームメートの行動は本当に私の神経を逆なでする。

Gary's the kind of person who likes to rub it in when he finds some fault in other people.

ゲーリーは、他人の欠点を見つけたらそれをわざと繰り返し言うのが好き、というタイプの人間だ。

If you and your husband really can't see eye to eye, you might consider marriage counseling.

もしあなたとご主人が本当に意見が合わないのなら、結婚カウンセリングを検討してもいいかもしれない。

You must sign up for at least 12 units in order to be considered a full-time student.

全日制の学生と見なされるためには、少なくとも 12 単位の（登録）申し込みをしなければならない。

No more cigarettes for me; I've turned over a new leaf.

タバコはやめた。心を入れ替えたんだ。

CD-A13

□ 193 **be cut out for ～**	**～に向いている** ≒ be suited to ～
□ 194 **boil down to ～**	**つまるところ～になる** ≒ be basically ～ ; be essentially ～
□ 195 **can't hold a candle to ～**	**～には及ばない**、～にはかなわない ≒ be not as good as ～
□ 196 **can't make heads or** [nor] **tails of ～**	**～を理解できない**、～がわからない ≒ can't understand ～ at all
□ 197 **find out ～ the hard way**	**身をもって学ぶ** ≒ learn ～ through a bad experience
□ 198 **run across ～**	**～を偶然見つける**、～にばったり出会う ≒ accidentally find ～ ; stumble upon ～
□ 199 **run for ～**	**～に立候補する** ≒ seek election to become ～
□ 200 **take ～ into account**	**～を考慮に入れる** ≒ consider

continued ▼

I guess I'm just not cut out for physics.	私は、物理学にはどうも向いていないようだ。
The reason you were selected for the job boils down to the fact that you had the most experience in the field.	あなたがその仕事に抜擢された理由は、つまるところ、その分野で最も経験があったということに行き着く。
Professor Emerson's recent work can't hold a candle to what he accomplished when he was younger.	エマーソン教授の最近の研究は、教授自身の若いころの功績には及ばない。
I couldn't make heads or tails of the chart John used in his presentation.	ジョンがプレゼンテーションで用いたチャートは、理解できなかった。
If Bill isn't nicer to his girlfriend, he'll find out the hard way how to treat a lady.	もしビルがガールフレンドに優しくないのなら、女性の扱い方を身をもって学ぶことになるだろう。
I ran across something very interesting when I was looking through some of my old records.	古いレコードの何枚かに目を通していた時、とても興味深いものを偶然見つけた。
Betty told me that she's thinking of running for the head of the student council again this year.	ベティーは、今年もまた生徒会長に立候補することを考えていると私に話した。
When I give you your final grade, I will also take your classroom participation into account.	最終評点を与える時には、授業への参加状況も考慮に入れるでしょう。

continued ▼

CD-A13(continued)

□201 take ～ with a grain of salt	**～を話半分に聞く**、～を割引して聞く ≒ treat [consider] ～ skeptically
□202 turn out ～	**結局～になる**、～であることがわかる ≒ conclude
□203 a whole lot more	**それ以上の**、十分以上の ≒ more than that
□204 day in and day out	**明けても暮れても** ≒ every day
□205 from time to time	**時々** ≒ occasionally
□206 in the nick of time	**ぎりぎりの時に**、際どい時に ≒ just before time ran out
□207 out of the question	**問題外で**、まったく不可能で ≒ not an option
□208 You can say that again!	**ごもっとも!**、その通り! ≒ That's for sure!

Tom's stories should always be taken with a grain of salt.

トムの話はいつも話半分で聞くべきだ。

I'm glad your job interview turned out so well.

就職の面接が結局とてもうまくいってよかったね。

Larry is a great athlete and a whole lot more; rumor has it that he's a fantastic cook, too.

ラリーは素晴らしい選手であるだけではない。うわさによると、素晴らしい料理人でもあるらしい。

Dan's been working on his new book day in and day out.

ダンは明けても暮れても新しい著作に取り組んでいる。

I wouldn't eat it every day, but from time to time Russian food sure is delicious.

毎日は食べないけれど、時々食べるロシア料理はとてもおいしい。

Irene made it to the hospital just in the nick of time; otherwise her baby would've been born in the taxi.

アイリーンは、ぎりぎり病院に間に合った。そうでなければ、彼女の赤ちゃんはタクシーの中で生まれるところだった。

It's out of the question for you to take on a part-time job until you get your grades up to an acceptable level.

許容できるレベルに成績が上がるまでは、アルバイトをするなんて問題外だ。

You can say that again; there's no doubt about it.

ごもっとも。それについては疑いの余地がない。

CD-A14

□209 **be a far cry from ～**	**～とは大違いだ**、～どころではない ≒ be quite different from ～
□210 **catch ～ red-handed**	**～を現行犯で捕まえる** ≒ discover ～ firsthand
□211 **catch up on ～**	**～の遅れを取り戻す** ≒ get up to date with ～
□212 **get the hang of ～**	**～のコツをつかむ** ≒ learn how to do ～
□213 **look high and low for ～**	**～をくまなく探す** ≒ search everywhere for ～
□214 **put one's mind to ～**	**～に全力を傾ける** ≒ concentrate on ～
□215 **serve ～ right**	**～には当然の報いだ** ・「ざまあみろ」「いい気味だ」というニュアンスがある。 ≒ be what ～ deserves
□216 **turn out to be ～**	**結局～になる** ≒ result in being ～

continued ▼

This small town sure is a far cry from the big city you grew up in, isn't it?

この小さな町とあなたが育った大都市では大違いに決まってますよね？

Howard was caught red-handed shoplifting at the convenience store down the street.

ハワードは通りを下ったところにあるコンビニで、万引きの現行犯で捕まった。

I'm afraid I can't go bowling with you tonight; I have to catch up on my reading for history class.

残念ながら、今夜は君とボウリングには行けないよ。歴史のクラスの読書課題の遅れを取り戻さなきゃならないんだ。

It takes at least three weeks for new students to get the hang of dormitory life.

新入生たちが寮生活のコツをつかむには、少なくとも3週間はかかる。

I've looked high and low for the new pen I bought last week, but it's nowhere to be found.

先週買った新しいペンを至る所探したが、どこにも見つからない。

If Barbara would put her mind to her studies the way she does to chasing boys, she'd get straight A's.

もしバーバラが、男の子を追い掛けるように勉強に全力を傾けたら、彼女はオールAを取れるだろう。

If you didn't pay the bill, it serves you right to have your electricity turned off.

もし料金を支払わなかったのなら、電気を止められるのは当然のことだ。

No matter how carefully we plan, things don't always turn out to be the way we expect them to be.

どんなに慎重に計画を立てても、物事は結局いつも期待通りになるとは限らない。

continued ▼

CD-A14(continued)

□217
as far as I know

私の知る限り
≒ according to my knowledge

□218
come to think of it

考えてみれば
≒ now that I consider it

□219
up in the air

未定で、よくわからなくて
≒ uncertain

□220
six of one and half a dozen of the other

五十歩百歩、似たり寄ったり
≒ either way is about the same

□221
the short end of the stick

不利な扱い、損な役割
≒ a disadvantage

□222
Half a loaf is better than none.

ないよりはましだ。
≒ Having a little of something is better than having nothing.

□223
No doubt about it.

間違いない。、疑う余地がない。
≒ No denying it.

□224
The bottom line is ～.

とどのつまり～だ。
≒ The main point is ～.

As far as I know, everyone must submit their applications by the end of this week.

私の知る限り、全員が今週末までに願書を提出しなければならない。

Come to think of it, I'm not sure I turned off the light in the kitchen before we left on vacation.

考えてみれば、休暇に出掛ける前に台所の電気を消したかどうかわからない。

I dislike having my future so up in the air; I wish I knew what I was going to do.

自分の将来がはっきりしないことが嫌だ。自分が何をすることになるかがわかるといいのに。

For me, it's six of one and half a dozen of the other whether we go by train or by car.

電車で行くか車で行くかは、私にとってはどっちでもいいことだ。

It seems like you always end up getting the short end of the stick.

君は結局いつも不利な扱いを受けることになるみたいだね。

I realize these seats aren't the best in the theater, but half a loaf is better than none.

これらの席がこの劇場で一番いい所ではないのはわかっているが、ないよりはましだ。

"Are you sure you're not applying to any graduate programs?" "No doubt about it! I've got to work."

「本当にあなたはどの大学院のプログラムにも申し込んでいないの？」「もちろんです！　働かなくちゃいけないんです」

The bottom line is that each person needs to sell 40 tickets in order to raise enough money for our new band uniforms.

とどのつまり、新しいバンドのユニホームのための十分なお金を工面するために、各人 40 枚のチケットを売らなきゃいけない。

CD-A15

☐225
not ring a bell

ピンとこない
≒ be unfamiliar

☐226
wind up ～

結局～になる、～であることがわかる
≒ eventually become ～

☐227
all thumbs

手先が不器用な
≒ clumsy; not skilled

☐228
on the cutting edge

最先端の
≒ the latest

☐229
out of one's mind

気が狂って
≒ crazy

☐230
up to one's neck

身動きが取れなくて
≒ buried; overloaded

☐231
for next to nothing

二束三文で、ただ同然で
≒ very cheaply

☐232
in ages

ずいぶんと長い間
≒ for a long time

continued ▼

I'm afraid that name doesn't ring a bell with me.

残念ながら、その名前は私にはピンとこない。

I took a wrong turn on the highway and wound up totally lost.

ハイウエーで道を間違えて、結局、完全に迷子になってしまった。

My sister is quite talented at making model cars, but I'm all thumbs when it comes to doing anything with my hands.

私の姉は本当に模型自動車を作る才能があるが、私は手を使った作業となると不器用だ。

This software is on the cutting edge of facial recognition technology.

このソフトウエアは、顔認識技術においては最先端のものだ。

Derek is out of his mind if he thinks I'll help him write his philosophy term paper.

もし私が哲学の期末リポートを書くのを手伝うとデレクが思っているとしたら、彼は気が狂っている。

Busy? I'm up to my neck in things that needed to be done yesterday!

忙しいかって？　昨日終わらせなきゃいけなかった件があって、身動きが取れないよ！

That new fast-food restaurant is selling hamburgers for next to nothing.

その新しいファストフード店は、ただ同然の値段でハンバーガーを売っている。

It looks like Bill hasn't worked out in ages. He's put on so much weight, I hardly recognized him!

ビルはずいぶん長い間運動をしていないようだ。かなり太ったのでほとんど彼とは気付かなかった！

continued ▼

CD-A15(continued)

□233 **over my dead body**	**絶対～させない**、決して～ない ≒ never
□234 **I couldn't agree more.**	**その通り。**、ごもっとも。 ≒ I agree totally.
□235 **Not on your life!**	**とんでもない！**、絶対に嫌だ！ ≒ I won't do it!
□236 **So far, so good.**	**今のところ順調である。** ≒ The progress is good.
□237 **Speak for yourself.**	**勝手なことを言わないでくれ。**、私は違う。 ≒ I don't feel the same as you.
□238 **The shoe is on the other foot.**	**立場が逆転している。** ≒ The roles are reversed.
□239 **You can bet on it.**	**間違いない。**、きっとだ。 ≒ It's certain.
□240 **You said it!**	**まったくその通り！** ≒ That's for sure!

My roommate will be borrowing my CDs again over my dead body!

ルームメートに再びCDを貸すことなんて絶対にない。

I couldn't agree more. That orchestra is one of the best I've ever heard.

その通りだね。そのオーケストラは、僕が今まで聞いた中で一番だ。

Not on your life! There's no way I'll do that.

とんでもない！　僕はそんなこと絶対にやらないよ。

So far, so good as far as my senior thesis is concerned. All I have left to do now is to proofread my final draft.

卒業論文に関していうと、今のところ順調だ。今やり残しているのは、最終原稿の校正だけだ。

Did you say Richard gets along with everyone? Speak for yourself! He does nothing but argue with me.

リチャードが皆と仲良くやってるって君は言ってたっけ？　勝手なことを言わないでくれ！　彼は私と口論しかしてないよ。

Gordon always yells at me to clean up the kitchen, but recently the shoe's been on the other foot.

ゴードンはいつも台所を掃除しろと私を怒鳴りつけているが、近ごろ立場が逆転してきている。

I'll be at the party tomorrow. You can bet on it.

私は明日のパーティーにいるよ。きっとね。

You said it! It sounds great to me, too.

まったくその通り！　私もそれが良いと思う。

復習テスト（Day 11-15）

（正解・訳例は pp.110-111）

1 赤字の意味としてもっともふさわしいものを A ～ D の中から選びなさい。

1. Grover's new sports car must have cost him an arm and a leg.

A. 全財産をはたかせる　B. 多額の出費である　C. 大した金額ではない　D. 身の丈に合った買い物である

2. "Can you come to the party I'm throwing next Friday, Whitney?" "Yeah, but I'll only have time to drop in on it, though."

A. あいさつする　B. 届け物をする　C. 通り過ぎる　D. ちょっと顔を出す

3. I can't believe Harry noticed the flaw in the professor's argument. He doesn't miss a beat, does he?

A. 優しくない　B. 協調性がない　C. ちゅうちょしない　D. 図々しい

4. Sam gets paid today and he said he would pick up the tab when we go out to eat tonight.

A. タクシーで迎えに行く　B. 勘定を持つ　C. お金持ちになる　D. 現金を引き出す

5. The school's tentative plan to lay off excess staff will only scratch the surface of the problem.

A. 解決に寄与する　B. 悪化させる　C. 人に知らしめる　D. 上面をなでる

6. Stop taking it out on me. It's not my fault.

A. 仲間外れにする　B. 悪く言う　C. 八つ当たりする　D. 真剣に受け止める

7. After this book project is finished, I'm going to take some time off to relax.

A. 外出する　B. 休みを取る　C. 家に帰る　D. 一人になる

8. I talked my sister out of marrying that man.

A. 説得してやめさせた　B. 説得して促した　C. 説得して検討させた　D. 説得して延期させた

9. The department head really seems to have it in for me. I wonder what she's got against me.

A. 遠慮している　B. ライバル視している　C. 馬鹿にしている　D. うらみを持っている

10. Darren has no money and no job. I'd say he definitely has two strikes against him when it comes to finding a girlfriend.

A. 2回失敗している　B. ピンチである　C. これからである　D. 見放されている

11. Welcome to our winery in Napa! Please help yourself to the wine.

A. ワインをご自由にお召し上がりください　B. ワインは持参してください
C. ワイン造りを学んでください　D. 好みのワインを選んでください

12. Pop music comes and goes so quickly that it's hard to keep up with what's in every year.

A. 覚えておく　B. 遅れずついていく　C. 予想する　D. すべて聞く

13. Top sales, six weeks in a row? I wonder how she pulled that off.

A. やり遂げた　B. でっち上げた　C. 目標にした　D. 継続させた

14. Professor Jackson really snapped at Carl this morning, but I think Carl rubs everyone the wrong way in that class.

A. 皆に誤解される　B. 皆の神経を逆なでする　C. 皆を利用する　D. 皆を無視する

15. I admit I made a mistake, but you don't have to rub it in.

A. 繰り返し言う　B. 馬鹿にする　C. 同情する　D. 尻ぬぐいをする

16. Are you going to sign up for Professor Smith's economics class next semester?

A. 受講料を支払う　B. 代理で登録する　C. 受講許可サインをもらう　D. 申し込む

17. Before you buy a car, you need to take the mileage into account.

A. 口座に入れる　B. 考慮する　C. 度外視する　D. 移しておく

18. As it turned out, Jack had been kicked out of school last year.

A. 取り消された　B. うわさになった　C. わかった　D. 説明された

19. "What did you get for winning the Mr. Olympia competition?" "Well, there was a medal, the trophy of course, and a whole lot more."

A. もっとたくさん　B. もう２～３点　C. それで十分　D. あとちょっとしたもの

20. I'm the only one in my family who has to listen to my sister's complaints day in and day out. It drives me nuts.

A. 気まぐれに　B. 時々　C. 来る日も来る日も　D. 午前と午後に

21. "Do you still hear from your old classmates from school?" "From time to time."

A. 時折　B. しょっちゅう　C. 数時間ごとに　D. ごくまれに

22. The firefighters arrived just in the nick of time to save the people inside the building.

A. 程なくして　B. 際どい時に　C. ひと足遅く　D. ずいぶんたって

23. The proposal for a new transfer system is so ridiculous that it is absolutely out of the question.

A. 問題外だ　B. 質問に値する　C. 問題の棚上げである　D. 疑わしい

24. "This humidity is terrible." "You can say that again! I'm already sweating."

A. もう一度言って　B. そうは思わない　C. その通り　D. しつこいな

25. As far as I know, no country has a better public transportation system than Japan.

A. 長年にわたって　B. 初めて耳にしたのだが　C. ご存じの通り　D. 私の知る限り

26. "I think it's been at least six months since we last met." "I agree. Come to think of it, it was last Christmas, actually."

A. 考えてみれば　B. 落ち着いてごらん　C. 一緒に考えよう　D. 考えられないことだけど

27. I want to go to Europe this summer but my plans are still up in the air.

A. 身の程知らずな　B. 未確定な　C. 中止になりそうな　D. 無駄な

28. I don't really care if the meeting is tomorrow or Friday. It's six of one and half a dozen of the other to me.

A. 日常茶飯事　B. すべて大切　C. 似たり寄ったり　D. 他人事

29. The new welfare program will leave poorer families with the short end of the stick.

A. 不利な立場　B. わずかな援助　C. 性急な議論　D. 対極の結論

30. This coat is too thin to offer much protection, but half a loaf is better than none in weather like this.

A. むしろ役に立つ　B. うってつけだ　C. あっても意味がない　D. ないよりはましだ

31. "Don't you think Lola is the most attractive woman in this class?" "No doubt about it."

A. 間違いない　B. 納得できない　C. 絶対に違う　D. 誰も賛成しない

32. The bottom line is that you need to spend more time studying.

A. 言い返すようだけど　B. 最初に　C. 結局のところ　D. 言い換えると

33. Every time I see a romantic movie, I wind up crying.

A. 泣く気がうせる　B. 泣くのをこらえる　C. 泣く羽目になる　D. 外に出て号泣する

34. "The food at the Italian restaurant is terrible." "Yeah, I couldn't agree more."

A. そうは思わない　B. 一理ある　C. その通り　D. 何とも言えない

35. "Dorothy, are you interested in going on a date with Susan's friend, Bob?" "Not on your life!"

A. 夢のようだ　B. お安いご用だ　C. 絶対に嫌だ　D. 都合がつけば

36. When Brad asked me about life in the new dorm, the only thing I could say was, "So far, so good."

A. 時間が解決する　B. 今のところ順調である　C. 最高に楽しい　D. 可もなく不可もない

37. "Everyone hated that movie!" "Speak for youself! I thought it was good."

A. もう一度言ってみろ　B. 皆そう思っている　C. 勝手なことを言うな　D. 胸の内を明かしてくれ

38. As soon as Virginia knew my secrets, the shoe was suddenly on the other foot in our relationship.

A. 立場が逆転した　B. ぎくしゃくした　C. 良くなった　D. 元通りになった

39. "Are you sure everybody will believe your story?" "You can bet on it."

A. その通り　B. 冗談だよ　C. そう願うよ　D. わからない

40. "That test was next to impossible!" "You said it! I couldn't even finish half of it."

A. 言わないで　B. とうとう言ったね　C. 頑張れ　D. その通り

2 類義表現を a ～ j の中から選びなさい。

1. beat around the bush
2. fall on hard times
3. get around to doing
4. grab a bite
5. have a way with words
6. have other fish to fry
7. knock oneself out
8. lose one's train of thought

- a. encounter financial difficulties
- b. find time to do
- c. forget what one planned to say
- d. work too hard
- e. talk indirectly
- f. use language skillfully
- g. have other interests
- h. take a break [vacation]
- i. fulfill a small amount
- j. quickly get something to eat

---

9. break the ice
10. go out on a limb
11. have a lot on one's mind
12. have it out
13. hit the nail on the head
14. keep in touch
15. see eye to eye
16. turn over a new leaf

- a. be really sharp; be on the ball
- b. be preoccupied
- c. be exactly right
- d. maintain contact
- e. consider
- f. create a relaxed atmosphere
- g. argue frankly
- h. change one's ways [habits]
- i. agree
- j. take a risk

17. be cut out for ~
18. boil down to ~
19. can't hold a candle to ~
21. can't make heads or [nor] tails of ~
20. find out ~ the hard way
22. run across ~
23. run for ~
24. take ~ with a grain of salt

a. treat [consider] ~ skeptically
b. dislike and want to harm ~
c. be basically ~; be essentially ~
d. accidentally find ~; stumble upon ~
e. be not as good as ~
f. register for ~
g. seek election to become ~
h. be suited to ~
i. learn ~ through a bad experience
j. can't understand ~ at all

---

25. be a far cry from ~
26. catch ~ red-handed
27. catch up on ~
28. get the hang of ~
29. look high and low for ~
30. put one's mind to ~
31. serve ~ right
32. turn out to be ~

a. maintain the same level with ~
b. be quite different from ~
c. learn how to do ~
d. visit ~ briefly
e. get up to date with ~
f. discover ~ firsthand
g. concentrate on ~
h. be what ~ deserves
i. result in being ~
j. search everywhere for ~

33. not ring a bell
34. all thumbs
35. on the cutting edge
36. out of one's mind
37. up to one's neck
38. for next to nothing
39. in ages
40. over my dead body

a. very cheaply
b. clumsy; not skilled
c. never
d. uncertain
e. occasionally
f. be unfamiliar
g. crazy
h. for a long time
i. buried; overloaded
j. the latest

復習テスト（Day 11-15）正解・訳例

1

1. B	2. D	3. C	4. B	5. D	6. C	7. B	8. A	9. D	10. B
11. A	12. B	13. A	14. B	15. A	16. D	17. B	18. C	19. A	20. C
21. A	22. B	23. A	24. C	25. D	26. A	27. B	28. C	29. A	30. D
31. A	32. C	33. C	34. C	35. C	36. B	37. C	38. A	39. A	40. D

1. グローバーの新しいスポーツカーは、彼にとってかなりの出費だったに違いない。
2. 「来週金曜に私が開くパーティーに来てくれる、ホイットニー？」「ええ、でも、ちょっと立ち寄るくらいの時間しかないけれど」
3. ハリーが教授の主張の不備を指摘したなんて信じられない。彼ってちゅうちょしないよね？
4. サムは今日給料日なの。で、今晩食事に出掛けたら自分が勘定を持つって、言ってたわ。
5. 余剰人員を一時解雇するという学校側の暫定案は、問題の上面をなでるだけだろう。
6. こっちにハつ当たりするのはやめて。私のせいじゃないわ。
7. この本のプロジェクトが終わったら、休暇を取ってリラックスするつもりだ。
8. 私は妹を説得して、その男との結婚をやめさせた。
9. 部署長は僕のことが本当に嫌いなようだ。僕の何が気に入らないのかな。
10. ダレンには金も仕事もない。恋人を見つけることにかけては、間違いなく不利な立場にいると思うね。
11. ナパの私たちのワイナリーにようこそ！　ご自由にワインをお飲みください。
12. ポピュラー音楽は移り変わりが激しいので、毎年の流行についていくのが大変だ。
13. 6週連続で売り上げトップですって？　彼女、どうやって達成したのかしら。
14. けさ、ジャクソン教授はカールに本当にきつく当たっていたけど、カールはあのクラスの皆の神経を逆なでしてると思うよ。
15. 過ちを犯したのは認めるが、それを何度も言わなくてもいいだろう。
16. 来学期、スミス教授の経済学のクラスに申し込むつもり？
17. 車を買う前に、燃費を考慮に入れる必要がある。
18. 後でわかったことだが、ジャックは去年退学になっていた。
19. 「ミスター・オリンピア・コンテストで優勝して、何をもらったの？」「ええと、メダルとトロフィーはもちろん、その他もろもろもらったよ」
20. 家族の中で、私だけが明けても暮れても姉の愚痴を聞かなくてはならない。本当に腹が立つよ。
21. 「学校のかつてのクラスメートからまだ便りがある？」「時々ね」

22. 消防士たちは際どいところで到着して、建物の中にいる人々を救出した。
23. その新しい振替制度の提案はひどくばかげているので、完全に問題外だ。
24. 「この湿気ときたらひどいね」「まったくだ！　もう汗が出てきてるよ」
25. 私の知る限り、日本ほど優れた公共交通機関を擁する国はない。
26. 「この前会ってから少なくとも6カ月はたっていると思うよ」「そうだね。考えてみれば、あれは実際去年のクリスマスだったな」
27. 今年の夏はヨーロッパに行きたいが、計画はまだ未定だ。
28. ミーティングが明日だろうが金曜だろうが構いやしない。私にとっては似たり寄ったりだ。
29. 新たな福祉制度では、貧困家庭は不利なままになるだろう。
30. このコートは薄過ぎてあまり役には立たないが、こんな天候では、ないよりはましだ。
31. 「このクラスでは、ローラが一番魅力的な女性だと思わない？」「それは間違いないね」
32. とどのつまり、君は勉強にもっと時間を割く必要がある。
33. 私は、恋愛映画を観るたびに泣く羽目になる。
34. 「あのイタリアン・レストランの料理はひどいね」「ああ、まったく同感だよ」
35. 「ドロシー、スーザンの友達のボブとデートする気ある？」「絶対に嫌よ！」
36. ブラッドに新しい寮での暮らしについて聞かれた時、「今のところは順調だよ」としか言えなかった。
37. 「あの映画は誰もが嫌ってたよ！」「勝手なこと言うなよ！　僕は素晴らしいと思ったぜ」
38. バージニアに秘密を知られた途端、私たちの関係において、突如として立場が逆転した。
39. 「皆があなたの話を信じてくれるって自信があるの？」「もちろん」
40. 「あのテスト、あり得ないよ！」「まったくだ！　半分も終わらなかった」

2

1. e	2. a	3. b	4. j	5. f	6. g	7. d	8. c	9. f	10. j
11. b	12. g	13. c	14. d	15. i	16. h	17. h	18. c	19. e	20. j
21. i	22. d	23. g	24. a	25. b	26. f	27. e	28. c	29. j	30. g
31. h	32. i	33. f	34. b	35. j	36. g	37. i	38. a	39. h	40. c

Chapter 2
頻出
イディオム
80

□ 241 **bear up**	**何とかやる**、〈負けないで〉頑張る ≒ handle the load; manage
□ 242 **blow a gasket**	**かんかんに怒る** ≒ become furious
□ 243 **doze off**	**うたた寝をする**、うとうとする ≒ involuntarily fall asleep
□ 244 **draw up ～**	～〈文書など〉**を作成する**、～〈計画〉を練る ≒ design; create
□ 245 **drive at ～**	**～を言おうとする**、～をほのめかす ≒ imply
□ 246 **get under way**	**開始する**、出発する ≒ start
□ 247 **go in for ～**	**～を好む**、～を趣味とする ≒ like to do ～
□ 248 **hit the hay**	**床に就く** ≒ go to bed

continued ▼

I really respect you for the way you're always able to bear up so well, even in the face of such direct criticism.	あれほどの直接的な批判にさらされていても、いつも何とかうまくやれるあなたを、私は本当に尊敬しています。
Boy, did William ever blow a gasket when he heard his girlfriend was seeing someone else!	参ったよ、ウィリアムは、自分のガールフレンドが誰かほかの人とつき合っていたと聞いてかんかんだったよ！
I must have dozed off during the end of the movie. How did it turn out?	映画の最後の方でうたた寝しちゃったに違いない。結局どうなったんだい？
Let's decide who will be responsible for drawing up the first draft of our proposal.	私たちの提案の、最初の原稿作成を誰が担当するのか決めよう。
Even if Brenda didn't come right out and say it, it was pretty clear to me what she was driving at.	たとえブレンダが思い切って言わなかったとしても、私には彼女が何を言おうとしていたかはかなり明白だった。
When do you expect we'll be able to get under way? If we don't leave soon, it'll be dark by the time we get there.	私たちはいつごろ出発できると思う？早く出発しなければ、そこに着くまでに暗くなってしまうよ。
Brian certainly has gone in for tennis in a big way, hasn't he?	ブライアンは、間違いなくテニスが大好きだったんだよね？
I've been working hard all day today. I'm going to hit the hay around 8 o'clock tonight.	今日は１日中一生懸命働いた。今夜は８時ごろに床に就くつもりだ。

continued
▼

CD-A16(continued)

□ 249 **hold one's horses**	**ちょっと待つ**、はやる心を抑える ≒ wait
□ 250 **hold up ～**	**～を遅らせる**、～を妨げる ≒ delay
□ 251 **iron out ～**	**～を円滑にする**、～〈相違・困難など〉を解消する ≒ smooth over ～; resolve
□ 252 **make out**	**うまくやる**、やっていく ≒ get along; fare
□ 253 **open up to ～**	**～と打ち解ける** ≒ share one's thoughts and feelings with ～
□ 254 **pull through**	〈困難・危険を〉**切り抜ける** ≒ recover; eventually be successful
□ 255 **tie the knot**	**結婚する** ≒ get married
□ 256 **wear off**	**徐々に減少する** ≒ gradually stop having an effect

If you can just hold your horses a few seconds while I finish eating, I'll be happy to help you do the dishes.

僕が食べ終わるまでほんのちょっとの間待っていられるのなら、喜んで皿洗いを手伝うよ。

What do you suppose is holding up the delivery of that package you sent me last week?

先週私に送ってくれた荷物の配達が遅れているのはどうしてだと思いますか。

Nancy and I have decided to sit down and try to iron out some of our differences.

ナンシーと私は腰をすえて、お互いの相違点のいくつかを解消しようと決めた。

Did you make out as well as you'd hoped during last week's contract negotiations?

先週の契約交渉の間、君が望んでいた通りにうまくやりましたか。

The more you get to know Carrie, the more willing she is to open up to you.

キャリーのことを知れば知るほど、彼女は進んであなたと打ち解けるようになるだろう。

Dan had his operation, and pulled through just fine.

ダンは手術を受けて､無事に切り抜けた。

Tina and Kevin have announced that they're going to tie the knot soon after they graduate.

ティナとケビンは、卒業後すぐに結婚するつもりだと発表した。

The doctor told me I should expect to experience some pain after the medication she gave me wears off.

医者は私に、渡した薬が切れてきたらある程度の痛みを感じるはずだ､と言った。

CD-A17

□257 **hit the ceiling**	**かんかんに怒る** ≒ become very angry
□258 **put ～ on**	**～をからかう** ≒ pull one's leg; trick
□259 **sit in for ～**	**～の代理をする** ≒ temporarily take the place of ～
□260 **stick up for ～**	**～をかばう**、～を弁護する ≒ defend; speak in support of ～
□261 **stick with ～**	**～**〈仕事など〉**を続ける** ≒ continue with ～; be diligent about ～
□262 **tap into ～**	**～を利用する** ≒ take advantage of ～; make use of ～
□263 **dirt cheap**	**非常に安い** • 副詞としても使われる。 ≒ very inexpensive
□264 **in hot water**	**困って**、面倒なことになって ≒ in trouble

continued ▼

You'll probably hit the ceiling when I tell you this, but I left your lecture notes out in the rain.	私がこれを話したらかんかんに怒るだろうけれど、君の講義メモを外の雨の中に置き忘れてしまったんだ。
You've got to be putting me on! There's no way Sam is only 35. He looks at least 50.	私をからかっているんだね！ サムがたった35歳なわけないでしょう。少なくとも50歳に見えるよ。
I'm going away for a week in August, and I asked Cheryl to sit in for me at the office.	8月に1週間、留守にするつもりなんだ。だから、シェリルに職場で私の代わりをしてくれるよう頼んだのさ。
In some cultures it's very important to stick up for members of your own family; no matter what they've done, you are obliged to support them.	一部の文化では、家族をかばうのはとても大事なことである。家族がどんなことをしたとしても、擁護しなければならないのだ。
If I were you, I'd stick with your present job until the economic future in your industry brightens a little.	もし私があなたなら、あなたの業界の経済的見通しが少し明るくなるまで現在の仕事を続けるだろう。
We had to tap into our savings to pay the rent this month.	私たちは今月、家賃を支払うのに貯金を切り崩さなければならなかった。
Camping equipment is dirt cheap at the army supply store on Marston Street.	マーストン通りの軍用供給店では、キャンプ用品は非常に安価だ。
It seems that Ken's procrastination has finally landed him in hot water with his boss.	ケンは、ぐずぐずしていたせいで、ついに上司との関係がまずくなってしまったようだ。

continued ▼

CD-A17(continued)

□265
in one piece

五体満足で
≒ uninjured

□266
off the hook

〈義務から〉**解放されて**、責任を免れて
≒ escape responsibility

□267
on one's way out

出る途中で
・one's の代わりに the が用いられることもある。
≒ leaving

□268
spick and span

小ぎれいな、ピカピカの
≒ extremely clean

□269
on the dot

時間きっかりに
≒ precisely at a certain time

□270
a white lie

罪のないうそ
≒ a minor, well-intentioned deception

□271
food for thought

考える材料、思考の糧
≒ thought-provoking ideas

□272
word of mouth

口コミ
≒ conversation; gossip

It's amazing you're still in one piece considering how fast you were going when you hit that tree yesterday.

昨日あなたが木にぶつかったときの速さを考えると、いまだに五体満足でいるのは驚くべきことだ。

It was nice of your boss to let you off the hook about working this weekend.

あなたを今週末の仕事から解放してくれるなんて、あなたの上司は親切でしたね。

I'm afraid I can't meet with you now, Lisa. I'm just on my way out.

残念ながら今は会えないよ、リサ。ちょうど出る途中なんだ。

Wow! Your house certainly is looking spick and span. Is the Queen of England coming to visit or something?

おや！　君の家は実に小ぎれいだね。英国女王陛下でも訪ねて来るか何かなの？

Make sure you're on time for your appointment with Sally. I guarantee you that she'll show up right on the dot.

サリーとの約束には、時間通りに行くようにしなさい。彼女が時間きっかりに現れることを保証するよ。

Telling a white lie is sometimes necessary to prevent a friend's feelings from being hurt too much by the naked truth.

罪のないうそをつくことは、ありのままの事実で友人の気持ちがひどく傷つくことを防ぐのに、時には必要なのです。

I'm not sure I agree with what you said, but your comments during class today certainly were food for thought.

あなたが言ったことに賛成するかどうかはわからないが、確かに今日の授業でのあなたの意見は考える材料になった。

The most effective advertising is word of mouth; what other people tell you makes more of an impression than what you see on television or read in a magazine.

最も効果的な宣伝は、口コミによるものだ。他の人から伝わる話は、テレビで見たり雑誌で読んだりするよりももっと強い印象を与える。

CD-A18

□273 **be like looking for a needle in a haystack**	**見つけるのが非常に困難だ**、無駄骨を折る ≒ be almost impossible
□274 **flunk out**	**成績不良で退学する** ≒ fail the program
□275 **get by**	**どうにかやっていく**、しのぐ ≒ survive
□276 **get carried away**	**調子に乗り過ぎる**、夢中になる ≒ be unable to control oneself
□277 **get one's own way**	**わがままを通す** ≒ have things how one wants them
□278 **get the lead out**	**さっさとやる** ≒ hurry up
□279 **get up on the wrong side of the bed**	**機嫌が悪い** ≒ be in a bad mood for no reason
□280 **have butterflies in one's stomach**	**どきどきする**、緊張する ≒ be nervous

continued ▼

Trying to find Joe Smith in the phone book will be like looking for a needle in a haystack.

電話帳でジョー・スミスを探そうとしても、見つけるのは困難だろう。

Nate did all of the course assignments, but he flunked out after failing all of his exams.

ネートは課題を全部こなしたが、すべての試験に落第して成績不良で退学になった。

How do you manage to get by on such a small scholarship?

そんなに少ない奨学金でどういうふうにしのいでいくんだい？

That rock concert was so exciting that many people in the audience got carried away dancing in front of the stage.

そのロックコンサートはとても刺激的だったので、観客の中の多くがステージの前で踊って羽目を外していた。

I think the reason why Tony always insists on getting his own way is because he was raised as an only child.

トニーがいつもわがままを通そうと主張するのは、彼が一人っ子で育ったからだと思う。

Let's go, Ralph. If you don't get the lead out, we'll never make it to class on time.

行こう、ラルフ。さっさとやらないと、僕たちは絶対に授業に間に合わないよ。

David must have gotten up on the wrong side of the bed this morning. He's being pretty hard on everybody he talks to.

デービッドは、けさ機嫌が悪かったに違いない。彼は、話す人皆にかなりきつく当たるんだ。

It's perfectly normal to have butterflies in your stomach before such a big football game.

こんなに大きなフットボールの試合の前に緊張するのは、極めて自然なことだよ。

continued ▼

□281 **have one's feet on the ground**	**地に足が着いている** ≒ be realistic
□282 **judge a book by its cover**	**見掛けで判断する** ≒ reach a conclusion based on appearance
□283 **keep on one's toes**	**油断しない**、身構えている ≒ stay alert
□284 **keep one's shirt on**	**冷静になる** ≒ be patient; calm down
□285 **leave no stone unturned** (doing)	(～しようと)**あらゆる手段を尽くす** ・捜し物の調査について使われることが多い。 ≒ investigate thoroughly
□286 **let the cat out of the bag**	**秘密を漏らす** ≒ publicize a secret
□287 **lose one's head**	**冷静さを失う**、かっとなる ≒ lose control; get angry
□288 **save one's breath**	〈無駄だと悟って〉**黙っている**、説得をやめる ≒ not waste one's effort

Rob is the kind of person who always has his feet on the ground; he never promises something he can't do.

ロブは、常に地に足が着いているタイプの人間だ。彼は、できないことは決して約束しない。

When it comes to Walter, be careful not to judge a book by its cover. He's much friendlier than he first seems.

ウォルターに関していえば、見掛けで判断しないよう注意してね。彼は最初に受ける印象よりずっとフレンドリーだよ。

Make sure you keep on your toes when you drive in Los Angeles. You never know what other drivers will do.

ロサンゼルスで車を運転するときは、油断しないようにしなさい。ほかのドライバーたちがどんなことをするか絶対にわからないんだから。

Keep your shirt on, Mister. I'm working as fast as I can.

冷静になってください。私は可能な限り急いでやっています。

Ivan still can't find his watch even though he says he's left no stone unturned looking for it.

アイバンは隅々まで捜したと言うけれど、まだ自分の腕時計を見つけることができない。

I wish you hadn't let the cat out of the bag about my relationship with Helen; I was trying to keep it a secret.

あなたが僕とヘレンの関係についての秘密を漏らさないでくれたらよかったのに。僕は、それを内緒のままにしようとしていたんだ。

I'd like to apologize to you for the way I lost my head last night over this month's telephone bill.

昨夜、今月の電話代に関してかっとなってしまったことを、君に謝りたいんだ。

Save your breath, Jim. Nothing you say will persuade me to go skiing this weekend.

無駄だからやめなさい、ジム。あなたが何を言っても今週末スキーに行くように私を説得するのは無理よ。

CD-A19

□ 289
bring ~ down to earth

~〈人〉を現実に引き戻す
≒ make ~ recognize reality

□ 290
bring ~ up to date

~〈人〉に最新情報を知らせる
≒ give ~ current information

□ 291
call ~ on the carpet

~を叱責する、〈叱責のため〉~を呼びつける
≒ criticize <a subordinate>; blame ~ officially

□ 292
fit ~ in

~を予定表に組み込む
≒ make room in the schedule for ~ ; find time for ~

□ 293
get ~ off one's chest

~を打ち明ける
≒ say ~ one had been holding back from saying

□ 294
get an early start on ~

~を早く始める
≒ begin doing ~ promptly

□ 295
have what it takes to be ~

~になる器がある
≒ possess the capability to be ~

□ 296
hear ~ firsthand

~をじかに聞く
≒ be told ~ directly

continued ▼

We all thought this class would be a snap, but that midterm test sure brought us all down to earth in a big hurry.

私たちは皆、この授業は朝飯前だと思っていたが、あの中間テストでまさしく急に現実へと引き戻された。

Could you bring me up to date on what's happening in this drama? I haven't seen any television in weeks.

このドラマで何が起こっているのか、最新情報を教えてくれる？ 何週間もまったくテレビを見ていないんだ。

The director of the institute called Harry on the carpet for failing to keep her informed of the results of his group's experiments.

研究所の所長は、グループの実験結果を報告し続けていなかったことについてハリーを叱責した。

Even if you don't have an appointment, I'll bet Professor Walters will be willing to fit you in somehow.

たとえあなたが面会の約束をしていないとしても、きっとウォルターズ教授はあなたを何とかして予定に入れるのをいとわないだろう。

I'm sorry I spoke so frankly, but I really had a few things I needed to get off my chest.

あまりにも率直に話してしまってごめんね、でも本当に打ち明けなくてはならないことがいくつかあったんだ。

The key to successfully passing this class is to get an early start on all the reading that needs to be done.

この授業をうまくパスする鍵は、終わらせなければいけない読書課題すべてを早くから始めることだ。

There's no question about it; Norman really has what it takes to be a successful businessman.

間違いない。ノーマンには、成功する実業家になる器が実際にある。

You can trust that information. I heard it firsthand from the president herself.

その情報は信用できるよ。社長である彼女自身からじかに聞いたから。

continued ▼

☐297
make a mountain out of a molehill

ささいなことを大げさに考える
≒ consider a minor problem to be serious

☐298
pay through the nose

法外なお金を払う
≒ pay an unfair price

☐299
play it by ear

臨機応変にやる
• it の代わりに things などが使われる場合もある。
≒ adjust one's actions to fit the situation

☐300
put all one's cards on the table

～の手の内を明かす
≒ reveal one's hidden thoughts frankly

☐301
rough it

不便な生活をする、自然のままの生活をする
≒ live without modern conveniences

☐302
start the ball rolling

率先して始める、〈話の〉口火を切る
≒ start something happening

☐303
throw cold water on ～

～に水を差す
≒ strongly discourage ～

☐304
turn one's back on ～

～を無視する、～に背を向ける
≒ forsake; ignore

Don't you think you might be making a mountain out of a molehill, Stacy? It's not that big a problem.	君はささいなことを大げさに考えているかもしれないとは思わないかい、ステーシー？　そんなに大した問題ではないよ。
Andy's car is really nice, but he's paying through the nose for it in monthly payments.	アンディーの車は本当にすてきだけれど、法外な金額を月々のローンで支払っているんだ。
Larry doesn't mind it at all when things don't go according to schedule; he's very adept at playing it by ear.	ラリーは、物事が予定通りに進まなくても全く気にしない。彼は、臨機応変にやるのがとても上手なんだ。
I wish you'd put all your cards on the table. I keep getting the feeling that you're holding something back.	あなたが手の内を明かしてくれたらなあ。あなたが何かを秘密にしているような気がずっとしているんだ。

Kay is so spoiled that her idea of roughing it is staying in a four-star hotel instead of a five-star one.	ケイはとても甘やかされているので、彼女にとって不便な生活をするというのは、五つ星ではなく四つ星ホテルに宿泊することなんだ。
If the district manager approves your proposal, we can start the ball rolling on its implementation right away.	地区支配人があなたの提案を認めてくれたら、直ちにその実現に向かって事を始めることができる。
Victor sure threw cold water on our proposal, didn't he? I was really excited about it until I talked to him.	ビクターは確実に僕たちの提案に水を差したんじゃない？　彼に話すまでは本当にわくわくしていたのに。
You shouldn't turn your back on your sister now; I think she really needs your advice this time.	今、お姉さんに背を向けるべきではない。今回は本当にあなたのアドバイスを必要としていると思うんだ。

CD-A20

□305 **better** (to be) **safe than sorry**	**転ばぬ先のつえ** ・後で後悔するよりは慎重にした方がいい、ということ。 ≒ wise to take precautions
□306 **down in the dumps**	**気が滅入って**、落ち込んで ≒ depressed
□307 **fit as a fiddle**	**ピンピンして**、非常に体調が良い ≒ healthy; in good condition
□308 **in seventh heaven**	**有頂天で** ≒ extremely happy
□309 **on pins and needles**	**そわそわして** ≒ anxious
□310 **out of the blue**	**突然に**、前触れもなく ≒ unexpectedly
□311 **straight from the horse's mouth**	**当人から直接**、確かな筋から ≒ firsthand
□312 **wide of the mark**	**的を外れて**、見当違いで ≒ inaccurate; wrong

continued ▼

Mark is the type of person who always believes it's better to be safe than sorry.

マークは、転ばぬ先のつえが大事だと常に考えるタイプの人間だ。

Why do you figure Darlene has been so down in the dumps recently?

ダーリーンが最近落ち込んでいるのはなぜだと思いますか。

I'm fit as a fiddle. I haven't felt better in years.

私は非常に体調が良い。ここ数年で一番良い。

Dave has been in seventh heaven ever since he got an A in his philosophy class last semester.

デーブは、先学期の哲学の授業でAを取って以来ずっと、うきうきしている。

Eric's on pins and needles waiting for the results of his CPA exam to come back.

エリックは、公認会計士の試験結果が戻ってくるのをそわそわして待っている。

Your resignation really has come out of the blue, Phil. Isn't there anything I can do to get you to stay on?

あなたの辞職は本当に突然のことです、フィル。あなたをとどまらせるために私にできることは何かないですか。

The reason I'm so sure that Carl is actually planning to move to Seattle is because I got it straight from the horse's mouth.

なぜカールが実際にシアトルに引っ越そうとしていることがはっきりわかるかというと、そのことをじかに聞いたからだ。

Your original assessment of Jane's potential was significantly wide of the mark; she's become a much better writer than you ever thought she'd be.

ジェーンの可能性についての君の最初の評価は、大変な見当違いだった。彼女は、君が思っていたよりずっと良い作家になった。

continued ▼

CD-A20 (continued)

□313 **a fly in the ointment**	**玉にきず**、興ざめ ≒ a problem with the plan
□314 **a piece of cake**	**朝飯前のこと**、簡単なこと ≒ easier than expected
□315 **A bird in the hand is worth two in the bush.**	**明日の百より今日の五十。** ・すでに手に入れたものの方がこれから手に入れようとするものより価値がある、ということ。≒ One sure thing is better than a possibility.
□316 **Every cloud has a silver lining.**	**苦は楽の種。** ・悪いことの半面には必ず良いこともある、の意。 ≒ Good things also come from bad situations.
□317 **It takes two to tango.**	**お互いさまだ。** ・タンゴを踊るには2人必要で1人では無理。そこから「お互いさま」の意になった。 ≒ Each side is to blame.
□318 **That's all for now.**	**それで差し当たりは十分だ。** ≒ That's enough for the present.
□319 **That's the way it is.**	**それが現実だ。**、そんなものだ。 ≒ That's the reality of the situation.
□320 **The more the merrier.**	**人は多ければ多いほど楽しい。** ≒ More people will be more fun.

The unexpected traffic jam on the freeway was a real fly in the ointment for their dinner date.

高速道路での思いがけない交通渋滞は、彼らのディナーのデートを本当に興ざめなものにした。

Climbing that mountain was a piece of cake — far easier than I expected it'd be.

あの山を登るのは朝飯前だった——私が予想していたよりもはるかに簡単だったんだ。

I think you should stay with the job you've got now, no matter how attractive the other offers seem to be. A bird in the hand is worth two in the bush.

たとえほかの申し出がどんなに魅力的に見えたとしても、あなたは今の仕事にとどまった方がいいと思う。明日の百より今日の五十だからね。

Even if something bad happens to Trudy, she always tries to remember that every cloud has a silver lining.

トルーディーは、たとえ何か悪いことが起こっても、いつも苦は楽の種ということを思い出そうとする。

Don't put all the blame on your roommate, Fred. It takes two to tango.

ルームメートばかりを責めてはいけないよ、フレッド。お互いさまだからね。

That's all for now, Craig. I'll call you if I need you for anything else.

それで差し当たりは十分だよ、クレーグ。何かほかに君を必要とすることがあれば電話するからね。

I know you don't like having to mow the lawn every Saturday, Tom, but that's the way it is.

君が毎週土曜日に芝を刈らなければならないことが気に入らないのはわかるよ、トム。でも、それが現実なんだよ。

If you want to ask your brother to come along, it's OK with me. The more the merrier, I always say.

もし君がお兄さんを連れてきたいなら、僕はそうしてもらって構わないよ。いつも言っているように、人は多ければ多いほど楽しいから。

復習テスト（Day 16-20）

（正解・訳例は pp.144-145）

1 赤字の意味としてもっともふさわしいものを A ～ D の中から選びなさい。

1. "Did you finish your reading assignment?" "I wish I could have. I actually dozed off while I was reading."

A. うたた寝をした　B. 連絡が入った　C. 邪魔が入った　D. 体調が悪かった

2. What kind of sports did you go in for while you were in college?

A. 好む　B. 見る　C. とりまとめる　D. 勧誘する

3. Hold your horses. I have something to tell you before you go.

A. こちらを向け　B. 注意しろ　C. 慌てるな　D. 急げ

4. I hope that Jeff and Sue can iron out their problems and get back together again.

A. 解決する　B. 公開する　C. 包み隠す　D. 意識する

5. "How did your test go, Lucy?" "Well, I'm afraid I made out poorly on it."

A. 問題が良くなかった　B. 準備不足だった　C. うまくいかなかった　D. 問題の量が多かった

6. Since we've just moved into the dorm, Billy and I haven't really opened up to each other yet.

A. 性格が似ている　B. 面識がある　C. 打ち解ける　D. 荷をほどく

7. Sarah was in critical condition for one month, but she somehow pulled through.

A. 楽しんだ　B. 我慢した　C. 持ちこたえた　D. 現状を維持した

8. My reaction went away as the medicine wore off.

A. 古くなった　B. 間隔が空いた　C. 徐々に切れた　D. 量が増えた

9. My boss hit the ceiling when I asked for a raise.

A. かんしゃくを起こした　B. ふさぎ込んだ　C. 立ち上がった　D. 反論した

10. Neil was just putting me on when he said the president was coming to my dormitory.

A. からかう　B. 励ます　C. 驚かせる　D. 期待させる

11. Would you mind sitting in for my secretary at the conference tomorrow?

A. 代理をする　B. 座らせる　C. 応援する　D. 味方になる

12. Michael stuck up for me when I was accused of stealing my roommate's purse.

A. そばに立った　B. 非難した　C. 怒らせた　D. かばった

13. If you stick with your job through this busy period, I'm certain things will get better.

A. 外注する　B. やり直す　C. 続ける　D. やめる

14. To create this innovative product, we had to tap into the experiences of our customers.

A. 整理する　B. 調査する　C. 蓄積する　D. 利用する

15. Mariah asked me if I had time to talk, but I was just on my way out of the room.

A. 仕事中　B. 出る途中　C. 留守中　D. 模様替えの最中

16. I didn't want Mark to feel guilty about what he'd done, so I told him a white lie and said that no one had even noticed.

A. 真実　B. 悪意のないうそ　C. しらじらしい冗談　D. うわさ

17. Trying to find a small boy in the crowd at a baseball game is like looking for a needle in a haystack.

A. 造作もないことだ　B. 協力が求められる　C. 非常に困難だ　D. たやすいこととは限らない

18. I have to apologize to you for the way I got carried away at the party the other day.

A. 遅刻した　B. 調子に乗り過ぎた　C. 心配をかけさせた　D. 参加できなかった

19. Carol is so used to getting her own way that she will get depressed if this plan of hers fails.

A. 突飛なこと　B. 我を通すこと　C. ゆっくりすること　D. 中途半端なこと

20. You'd better watch what you say to Sandra today. She must have gotten up on the wrong side of the bed this morning.

A. 寝違えた　B. 体調が優れなかった　C. 寝坊をした　D. 虫の居所が悪かった

21. He may look like a janitor, but actually he's the chancellor of our university. You can't judge a book by its cover.

A. 医者の不養生　B. 坊主憎けりゃけさまで憎い　C. 人は見掛けによらぬもの　D. 五十歩百歩

22. I'll leave no stone unturned until I find the paycheck I misplaced.

A. 誰のせいにもしない　B. 全力を尽くす　C. 文句を言わずやり過ごす　D. 希望を持って対処する

23. I hope I didn't let the cat out of the bag when I told Jerry that you're thinking about leaving the company.

A. 冷静さを保つ　B. 規則を破る　C. 動揺する　D. 秘密を漏らす

24. The most important thing to do in the event of fire is to remain calm. Losing your head is the worst thing you can do.

A. 気を失う　B. 身を危険にさらす　C. 無視する　D. 慌てる

25. I heard the news firsthand from my mother, and it shocked me.

A. 初めて聞いた　B. 直接聞いた　C. 後で聞いた　D. 電話で聞いた

26. You shouldn't take what Mark says so seriously. He's just making a mountain out of a molehill.

A. 大げさに考える　B. 自意識過剰である　C. 大ぼらを吹く　D. 独り善がりである

27. I paid through the nose to get my pickup truck fixed and it still doesn't run properly.

A. 法外なお金を払った　B. ローンを組んだ　C. 職を失った　D. 一生懸命働いた

28. Virginia prefers to stick to a carefully prepared plan, whereas Eric is more flexible and tends to play things by ear.

A. 聞いて理解する　B. 臨機応変にやる　C. マイペースを守る　D. 中途半端にやる

29. Come on, don't hide anything Patricia. Put all your cards on the table.

A. 言うことを聞けよ　B. あきらめろよ　C. 落ち着いてくれよ　D. 手の内を見せろよ

30. While my apartment was being renovated, I roughed it in a tent set up in the backyard.

A. 家具を一式そろえた　B. 難儀した　C. 不便な生活をした　D. 体を壊した

31. Maybe I can start the ball rolling on this discussion, since my team has been working on this problem the longest.

A. 口火を切る　B. 進行役を指名する　C. 休憩を入れる　D. 議題から外れる

32. Robin is so crazy about the Beatles that she seems to have turned her back on all other forms of music.

A. 懐かしんだ　B. 無視した　C. 楽しんだ　D. 忘れた

33. Judy's grandpa turned 90 this March, but he's still fit as a fiddle.

A. 非常に元気だ　B. 薬を服用している　C. 気難しい　D. 分別がない

34. Driving to L.A. sounds great, but the fly in the ointment is that I've lost my license.

A. 興ざめ　B. 想定外　C. 秘密　D. 笑い話

35. "Wendy's Pizza offered me a job, but I may try to find a better one." "I think you should go for Wendy's. A bird in the hand is worth two in the bush."

A. どこにでも機会はある　B. これが運命というものだ　C. 気が変わるかもしれない　D. 確実なものを取った方がよい

36. Anna's philosophy of life is, "Every cloud has a silver lining," and she tries not to complain about anything.

A. 危険はどこにでも潜んでいる　B. 火のないところに煙は立たない
C. どんな悪いことにも良い側面がある　D. 努力はいつか報われる

37. "I got in a fight with Jim because he called me an idiot." "Yes, but it takes two to tango, as people say."

A. 時間が解決する　B. どっちもどっち　C. 明日があるさ　D. 口は災いのもと

38. "Have you finished your homework?" "Yes, that's all for now."

A. これでは物足りない　B. とりあえず全部　C. 予定どおり　D. 気が済むまでやった

39. I know you don't like the dorm rules, Bill, but that's just the way it is around here.

A. 規則はそれしかないのさ　B. それは表面上さ　C. それが現実さ　D. それは考え方次第さ

40. "How many people should we invite to the potluck party?" "The more the merrier."

A. 何人でもいい　B. 限定した方がいい　C. 多いほどいい　D. 知っている人の方がいい

2 類義表現を a ～ j の中から選びなさい。

1. bear up
2. blow a gasket
3. draw up ～
4. drive at ～
5. get under way
6. hit the hay
7. hold up ～
8. tie the knot

a. delay
b. become furious
c. publicize a secret
d. design; create
e. go to bed
f. get married
g. handle the load; manage
h. start
i. imply
j. involuntarily fall asleep

---

9. dirt cheap
10. in hot water
11. in one piece
12. off the hook
13. spick and span
14. on the dot
15. food for thought
16. word of mouth

a. very inexpensive
b. escape responsibility
c. in trouble
d. extremely clean
e. thought-provoking ideas
f. a problem with the plan
g. precisely at a certain time
h. conversation; gossip
i. leaving
j. uninjured

17. flunk out
18. get by
19. get the lead out
20. have butterflies in one's stomach
21. have one's feet on the ground
22. keep on one's toes
23. keep one's shirt on
24. save one's breath

a. foresake; ignore	b. be patient; calm down
c. become very angry	d. fail the program
e. hurry up	f. survive
g. stay alert	h. not waste one's effort
i. be nervous	j. be realistic

---

25. bring ～ down to earth
26. bring ～ up to date
27. call ～ on the carpet
28. fit ～ in
29. get ～ off one's chest
30. get an early start on ～
31. have what it takes to be ～
32. throw cold water on ～

a. defend; speak in support of ～
b. make ～ recognize reality
c. begin doing ～ promptly
d. criticize〈a subordinate〉; blame ～ officially
e. give ～ current information
f. say ～ one had been holding back from saying
g. strongly discourage ～
h. like to do ～
i. make room in the schedule for ～; find time for ～
j. possess the capability to be ～

33. better (to be) safe than sorry
34. down in the dumps
35. in seventh heaven
36. on pins and needles
37. out of the blue
38. straight from the horse's mouth
39. wide of the mark
40. a piece of cake

a. anxious
b. extremely happy
c. depressed
d. a minor, well-intentioned deception
e. firsthand
f. inaccurate; wrong
g. unexpectedly
h. healthy; in good condition
i. easier than expected
j. wise to take precautions

復習テスト（Day 16-20）正解・訳例

1

1. A	2. A	3. C	4. A	5. C	6. C	7. C	8. C	9. A	10. A
11. A	12. D	13. C	14. D	15. B	16. B	17. C	18. B	19. B	20. D
21. C	22. B	23. D	24. D	25. B	26. A	27. A	28. B	29. D	30. C
31. A	32. B	33. A	34. A	35. D	36. C	37. B	38. B	39. C	40. C

1. 「読書の課題終わらせた？」「そうだったらいいんだけど。実は、読んでるうちにうたた寝しちゃったの」
2. 大学の時、どんなスポーツが好きだった？
3. 落ち着いて。出発する前に君に伝えなきゃいけないことがあるんだ。
4. ジェフとスーが問題を解決して、またよりを戻せるといいけれど。
5. 「試験はどうだった、ルーシー？」「そうね、残念なことにうまくいかなかったの」
6. ビリーと私は寮に入ったばかりなので、まだお互いにあまり打ち解けていない。
7. サラは1カ月危篤状態にあったが、なんとか持ちこたえた。
8. 薬の効き目が切れてくるにつれて、副作用がなくなった。
9. 私が昇給を求めると、上司はかんかんに怒った。
10. ニールは、学長が僕の寮に来ると言って、僕をからかった。
11. 明日の会議で僕の秘書の代わりを務めてもらえるかな？
12. ルームメートの財布を盗んだと私が責められた時、マイケルは私をかばってくれた。
13. 君がこの忙しい時期に仕事をやり続ければ、事態はきっと好転するだろう。
14. この革新的な製品を作るために、われわれは顧客の経験を利用しなければならなかった。
15. 話をする時間があるかマライアに聞かれたが、私はちょうど部屋を出るところだった。
16. マークには取った行動をやましく思ってほしくなかったので、私は、誰も気付きさえしなかったと、罪のないうそをついた。
17. 野球の試合の人ごみの中で小さな男の子を見つけようとするのは、至難の業だ。
18. 先日、パーティーで調子に乗り過ぎたことを、君に謝らなくてはならない。
19. キャロルはわがままを通すのに慣れっこになっているので、自分のこの計画が駄目になったら落ち込むだろう。
20. 今日はサンドラに言うことには気を付けた方がいい。彼女は、けさ、機嫌が悪かったはずだよ。
21. 彼は用務員みたいに見えるかもしれないけど、実はうちの大学の学長なんだ。人は見掛けによらないね。

22. 置き忘れた給料支払い小切手を見つけるまで、僕は全力を尽くすつもりだよ。
23. ジェリーに、君が会社を辞めようかと思っているって話しちゃったけど、秘密を漏らさなきゃよかったよ。
24. 火災が発生したときに最も重要なのは、冷静でいることだ。最悪なのは、冷静さを失うことだ。
25. 私はその知らせを母からじかに聞いて、ショックを受けた。
26. マークの言うことをあまり真剣に受け取るべきじゃない。彼はささいなことを大げさに考えているだけだ。
27. 小型トラックを修理してもらうのに法外な金を払ったが、そのトラックはいまだにまともに走らない。
28. バージニアは用意周到な計画にこだわりたがる一方、エリックはもっと柔軟性があって、臨機応変にやる傾向がある。
29. ほらほら、隠し事はなしよ、パトリシア。手の内を明かしなさい。
30. アパートが改装中だった間、私は裏庭に張ったテントで不便な生活をした。
31. この問題に一番長く取り組んできたのは私のチームなので、私がこの議論の口火を切ってもいいだろう。
32. ロビンはビートルズにすっかり夢中で、ほかのあらゆる形式の音楽に背を向けてしまったようだ。
33. ジュディーの祖父はこの 3 月で 90 歳になった。でも彼はまだピンピンしている。
34. ロサンゼルスにドライブというと楽しそうに聞こえるが、興ざめなことに私は免許証をなくしてしまった。
35. 「ウェンディーズ・ピザで仕事の口がもらえたけど、もっといい口を探すかもしれない」「ウェンディーズの仕事をやるべきだと思うな。明日の百より今日の五十だよ」
36. アンナの人生哲学は「苦は楽の種」。それで、彼女は何事にも不平を言わないようにしている。
37. 「僕をばか呼ばわりしたので、ジムとけんかになったんだ」「ああ、でも、一般的に言われるように、お互いさまだよね」
38. 「宿題終わらせちゃった？」「うん、とりあえずね」
39. あなたが寮の規則を気に入らないのは知ってるわ、ビル。でも、ここいらじゃそんなものなのよ。
40. 「ポットラック・パーティー（料理などを持ち寄って行うパーティー）には何人招待しようか？」「人は多ければ多いほど楽しいよ」

2

1. g	2. b	3. d	4. i	5. h	6. e	7. a	8. f	9. a	10. c
11. j	12. b	13. d	14. g	15. e	16. h	17. d	18. f	19. e	20. i
21. j	22. g	23. b	24. h	25. b	26. e	27. d	28. i	29. f	30. c
31. j	32. g	33. j	34. c	35. b	36. a	37. g	38. e	39. f	40. i

Chapter 3

重要
イディオム
80

□ 321 **act up**	**いたずらする**、〈機械などが〉調子が狂う ≒ misbehave
□ 322 **come along**	**順調に進む**、進歩する ≒ progress
□ 323 **contain oneself**	**自制する** ≒ control one's emotion
□ 324 **count for ～**	**～の価値がある** ≒ be worth ～ ; represent
□ 325 **cut class**	**授業をさぼる** ≒ skip a lesson
□ 326 **dish out ～**	**～をばらまく**、～を配る、～(罰・批判など)を与える • dish it out で「こっぴどくしかる」の意。 ≒ give ～ liberally
□ 327 **foot the bill**	**勘定を持つ** ≒ pay
□ 328 **get cold feet**	**おじけづく** ≒ have second thoughts; hesitate

continued ▼

I need to go home a little early. My babysitter called to tell me my son has been acting up this afternoon.

少し早めに家に帰らなくてはなりません。息子が午後ずっといたずらをしている、とベビーシッターが電話をしてきたのです。

I'm glad to hear that the construction of the new student union building is coming along according to plan.

新しい学生会館の建設が予定通り順調に進んでいると聞いてうれしいよ。

They couldn't contain themselves when they met again after 10 years apart, and both burst into tears.

彼らは、10年離れ離れになって再会した時、気持ちを抑えることができずお互い涙があふれた。

Your final exam counts for 25 percent of your final mark in this class.

最終試験は、この授業の最終評点の5%を占めます。

I wanted to cut class yesterday because I felt so sick.

昨日は、気分がひどく優れなかったので、授業をさぼりたかった。

I guess Professor Thomas wasn't happy with our essays. I've never heard a teacher dish out as much criticism as he did today in class.

トーマス教授は僕たちの小論文に満足していなかったと思うよ。今日の授業で彼がしたほどの批判をこれまで教師がするのは聞いたことがない。

So, who's going to foot the bill for your summer trip to Canada?

で、誰があなたの夏のカナダ旅行の費用を持つつもりなの？

Julie was supposed to get married yesterday, but her fiancé got cold feet at the last minute and walked out on her.

ジュリーは昨日結婚することになっていたが、彼女の婚約者は土壇場でおじけづいて、彼女の元を去った。

continued ▼

□ 329
go off

〈話などに関して〉**脇道にそれる**
≒ digress

□ 330
kick the habit

〈悪習を〉**やめる**
≒ quit

□ 331
picture oneself doing

自分が～するのを想像する
• doing の部分には、過去分詞や節などが入ることもある。
≒ imagine oneself doing

□ 332
pull over

〈車などを〉**脇に寄せる**
≒ stop by the side of the road

□ 333
smell a rat

怪しいと思う、変だと気付く
≒ think something deceitful is happening

□ 334
take a dip

ひと泳ぎする
≒ go swimming

□ 335
wait on ～

～に仕える、～に給仕する
≒ serve

□ 336
walk out

ストライキをする
≒ go on strike; break off discussions

You may disagree, but I like the way Professor Barnes sometimes **goes off** and talks about things not directly related to the topic.

君は賛成しないかもしれないけど、私は、バーンズ教授がときどき脇にそれて論題に直接関係ないことを話すやり方が好きだ。

I think I've finally **kicked the habit**. I haven't smoked in two months.

私はついにやめられたと思う。もう2カ月もタバコを吸っていないよ。

I can't **picture myself** ever **getting** married.

結婚することなんて、僕には想像もできないな。

I think the siren and flashing lights might indicate that the patrol car behind us wants you to **pull over**, Helen.

サイレンとライトということは、後ろのパトカーがあなたに車を脇に寄せてほしいということかもしれないよ、ヘレン。

While my wife was on maternity leave, someone told her the company was interviewing people for a new position; I **smell a rat**.

妻が産休を取っている間、誰かが彼女に、会社は新しいポジションに就く人材の面接をしているって言ったんだ。僕は変だと思う。

The weather's pretty nice today. What do you think about **taking a dip** in the lake before lunch?

今日はとても天気がいいね。昼食前に湖でひと泳ぎしない？

Rick got a job **waiting on** tables over at the diner on Juniper Avenue.

リックは、ジュニパー街の食堂で給仕の仕事を得た。

The teachers are thinking about **walking out**; we may get a long summer vacation, after all!

先生たちがストライキをすることを考えている。ということはつまり、私たちは長い夏休みをもらえるかもしれない！

CD-A22

□ 337 **give off ～**	**～**〈蒸気・ガス・においなど〉**を放出する**、～を発する ≒ send out ～
□ 338 **hang onto ～**	**～を維持する**、～を保持する ≒ keep; not throw away
□ 339 **poke fun at ～**	**～をからかう** ≒ tease
□ 340 **stamp out ～**	**～を撲滅する**、～を撤廃する ≒ eliminate ～ totally
□ 341 **in a bind**	**困って**、焦って ≒ in a difficult situation
□ 342 **null and void**	〈法律的に〉**無効の** ≒ not legally binding; invalid
□ 343 **on the blink**	**故障して** ≒ not working properly
□ 344 **on the house**	**店のおごりで**、無料で ≒ provided free

continued ▼

I wonder if I did anything to make Beverly angry with me; she's been giving off strange non-verbal signals for about two weeks now.

私が何かビバリーを怒らせることをしたのかなあ。彼女はもう２週間近くも、おかしなしぐさや表情をしている。

Herman keeps optimistically hanging onto his old clothes, even though he'll never likely be able to fit into them again.

ハーマンは、たぶん二度とぴったり合うことはなさそうだけれど、どうにか使えると古い洋服を持ち続けている。

Don't take Oliver so seriously. He just enjoys poking fun at life in general.

オリバーの言うことをまじめに取っちゃ駄目だよ。彼はただ、人生全般をからかって楽しんでいるだけなんだ。

The new government has promised to stamp out corruption, but I'm not holding my breath waiting for it to happen.

新しい政府は汚職を撲滅することを約束したが、私はそれが実現するなんて期待していない。

You look like you're in a bind right now. Let me know if there's anything I can do to help.

今困っているようですね。何か私にお手伝いできることがあれば教えてください。

Because Frank was under 18 when he signed, the contract was declared null and void by the judge.

フランクはサインした時18歳未満だったので、その契約書は裁判官によって無効と公言された。

My microwave oven is on the blink again. Maybe I should just go ahead and buy a new one.

電子レンジがまた壊れている。たぶん思い切って新しいのを買うべきなんだろう。

Last night was the owner's birthday, so between five and six all drinks were on the house.

昨夜はオーナーの誕生日だったので、５時～６時の間は、飲み物がすべて無料だった。

continued
▼

CD-A22(continued)

□ 345 **for a song**	**ただ同然で**、捨て値で ≒ very cheaply
□ 346 **off the cuff**	**即座に**、即興で ≒ without preparation; spontaneously
□ 347 **on second thought**	〈考え直した結果〉**やっぱり** ≒ upon reconsidering
□ 348 **on the tube**	**テレビで** ≒ on television
□ 349 **a slap in the face**	**侮辱**、非難 ≒ an insult
□ 350 **a snow job**	**うそ**、口先だけの話 ≒ a false story
□ 351 **bread and butter**	**生活の糧**、主要な収入源 ≒ means of livelihood
□ 352 **Break a leg.**	**幸運を祈る。**、頑張れ。 ≒ Good luck!

I can't wait to see your new evening gown. Your roommate told me you picked it up for a song.

君の新しいイブニングドレスを見るのが待ち切れないよ。ただ同然で手に入れたって、君のルームメイトが教えてくれたんだ。

The politician really isn't very good at speaking off the cuff.

その政治家は本当のところ、即興で話すということがあまり得意ではない。。

I was going to go to the football game, but on second thought I think I'll stay home and watch it on television.

フットボールの試合に行くつもりだったけれど、やっぱり家にいてテレビで観戦しようと思う。

All Doug seems interested in these days is just sitting on his couch watching whatever's on the tube.

最近のダグときたら、ソファにただ座ってひたすらテレビを見ることにしか興味がないみたいなんだ。

Considering your GPA and recommendation letters, I think it's a real slap in the face that the graduate school decided not to accept you.

あなたのGPA(学業平均値。Grade Point Average)と推薦状のことを考えると、大学院があなたを受け入れないと決めたのは、本当に納得できないことだと思う。

Seth tried to pull a snow job on his English teacher by pretending to have read books he hadn't really read.

セスは、本当は読んでいない本を読んだと偽って、英語の先生をあざむこうとした。

He makes a good speech, but then as a politician, speech-making is his bread and butter.

彼は演説の名手だが、政治家としては、演説が彼にとっての生活の糧になっている。

I heard you're going out on a date with Bruce. Break a leg. I hope you have a good time.

ブルースとデートに出掛ける予定だって聞いたよ。幸運を祈る。楽しんできなよ。

CD-A23

□ 353
be lost in thought

物思いにふけっている
≒ be thinking deeply

□ 354
call in sick

病気で休むと電話をする
≒ contact someone to advise that one cannot work due to illness

□ 355
feel like a million dollars

最高の気分である
≒ feel great

□ 356
get in the way

邪魔する、妨害する
≒ be an obstacle

□ 357
get into a rut

マンネリ化する
≒ follow the same dull routine

□ 358
get on one's nerves

かんに障る、神経に障る
≒ irritate one

□ 359
get the cold shoulder

あしらわれる、断られる
≒ be treated indifferently

□ 360
get the show on the road

事を始める、活動を開始する
• the show の代わりに this show とも言う。
≒ begin

continued ▼

Sorry, I didn't catch what you were saying; I was lost in thought.

ごめん、君が言ってたことが聞き取れなかった。物思いにふけっていたんだ。

Mr. Henderson called in sick this morning, so can you please take his calls for today?

ヘンダーソンさんから、けさ、病気で休むと電話があったので、今日は彼の電話を代わりに取ってくれませんか。

You look great! I'll bet you feel like a million dollars now that you're working out regularly.

元気そうだね！ 定期的に運動しているから、きっととてもいい気分なんだね。

I've agreed to play baseball this term as long as it doesn't get in the way of my classwork.

今学期、教室学習の邪魔にならない限り野球をすることを承諾した。

Charlene says she's gotten into a rut at home the last few months, doing the same thing day after day.

シャーリーンは、来る日も来る日も同じことをして、ここ 2、3 カ月は家での生活がマンネリ化してしまったと言う。

Susan's arrogant attitude really gets on my nerves.

スーザンの高慢な態度は、本当にかんに障る。

The reason Kathleen didn't join the theater group was because she got the cold shoulder from some of the members.

キャスリーンがその劇団に加わらなかった理由は、メンバーの何人かに断られたからだった。

It's time for us to get the show on the road. We've been sitting here discussing what to do for more than an hour!

活動を開始する時間だ。私たちはここに座って 1 時間以上も何をするか話し合っているんだし！

continued ▼

CD-A23 (continued)

□ 361 **get under one's skin**	**～をいらいらさせる** ≒ irritate one
□ 362 **have ants in one's pants**	**そわそわしている** ≒ be restless; be impatient
□ 363 **have one's head in the clouds**	**空想にふける**、上の空でいる ≒ be unrealistic [dreamy]
□ 364 **hear oneself think**	〈騒々しい中で〉**落ち着いて考える**、集中する ≒ concentrate (amid noise)
□ 365 **jack up the price**	**値段を不正につり上げる** ≒ raise the price unfairly
□ 366 **keep a straight face**	**真顔でいる**、笑いをこらえる ≒ refrain from laughing
□ 367 **let one's hair down**	**くつろぐ**、羽を伸ばす ≒ have fun without worrying about what others think
□ 368 **put one's foot in one's mouth**	**まずいことを言う**、口を滑らせる ≒ say something inappropriate

The way some of the debate club members act really gets under my skin; I'm thinking of quitting.	討論クラブのメンバー数人のやり方には本当にいらいらする。私は辞めることを考えている。
You have ants in your pants today, Travis. I don't think I've ever seen you so impatient.	今日はそわそわしているね、トラビス。今までそんなにせっかちな君を見たことがない気がする。

Gary has his head in the clouds if he really thinks he'll get that scholarship he's applied for.	ゲーリーは、自分が申し込んだ奨学金を得られると本当に思っているとすれば、空想にふけっているということだよ。
The teacher yelled that she couldn't hear herself think and made all the children sit down.	先生は、(うるさくて) 集中することができないと叫んで、子供たちを全員座らせた。

This new trade agreement is just an excuse to allow auto manufacturers to jack up the prices on the cars they sell.	この新しい貿易協定は、自動車メーカーが車の販売価格を不正につり上げるのを許す口実にすぎない。
How in the world did you manage to keep a straight face when you asked your mother for extra money this month?	お母さんに今月余分なお金をねだるとき、いったいどうやってまともな顔をしていられたの？

Let's let our hair down and really have a good time tonight!	羽を伸ばして、今夜は心から楽しもうよ！
Shirley really put her foot in her mouth when she said she didn't like the painting. She didn't know she was talking to the artist himself.	シャーリーがその絵が好きではないと言ったのは本当にまずかった。彼女はその画家自身に話していたことを知らなかった。

CD-A24

□369
be head and shoulders above ～

～よりもはるかに優れている
≒ be far better than ～

□370
bite the hand that feeds ～

恩をあだで返す
≒ attack the source of one's support

□371
give ～ one's walking papers

～を解雇する、～と別れる
≒ fire; lay ～ off

□372
go off the deep end with ～

～にはまり込む、～にのめり込む
≒ become obsessed with ～

□373
have an ear for ～

～〈音楽、言葉など〉**のセンスがある**
≒ have a natural understanding of ～

□374
make a clean breast of ～

～を白状する、～を残らず打ち明ける
≒ honestly account for ～

□375
make money hand over fist

ぼろもうけする
≒ make a lot of money

□376
meddle in ～

～に干渉する、～に口を出す
≒ get involved in ～

continued ▼

Congratulations! Professor Klein told me your term paper was head and shoulders above any of the other ones he read.

おめでとう！ クライン教授が、あなたの期末リポートは、自分が目を通したそのほかの期末リポートのどれよりもずっと優れているって私に話してくれたよ。

Brenda is always getting into fights with her father. She probably doesn't realize she's biting the hand that feeds her.

ブレンダは、いつも父親とけんかになっている。彼女はたぶん、恩をあだで返していることに気づいていない。

It's about time the boss gave Winston his walking papers. He hasn't done a decent day's work since the day he was hired.

上司がウィンストンを解雇するのは、時間の問題だ。彼は雇われた日からきちんとした仕事をしていない。

Terry's really gone off the deep end with this new girl he's met.

テリーは、新しく出会った女の子に本当にのめり込んでしまった。

Linda's pronunciation of Swahili is very authentic; she must really have an ear for languages.

リンダのスワヒリ語の発音は、まさに本物だ。彼女には言語のセンスがあるに違いない。

I think you should go to Professor Davidson and make a clean breast of the real reason why you didn't submit your paper before the deadline.

君はデービッドソン教授のところに行って、締め切り前に論文を提出しなかった本当の理由を残らず打ち明けた方がいいと思う。

Kim's days of making money hand over fist are long gone. The recession has hit her company especially hard.

キムがぼろもうけできていた日々はとうの昔に過ぎ去ったよ。景気後退は彼女の会社に特に深刻な打撃を与えている。

I told you not to meddle in other people's affairs; let them sort out their problems on their own.

他人事に首を突っ込むなって言ったじゃないか。彼らの問題は彼らに解決させてやれよ。

continued ▼

CD-A24(continued)

□ 377 **not get a wink of sleep**	**一睡もしない** ≒ not sleep at all
□ 378 **pound the pavement**	〈仕事を探して〉**歩き回る** ≒ make genuine effort to find a job
□ 379 **rake ～ over the coals**	**～をしかりつける**、～に大目玉を食らわす ≒ criticize ～ severely
□ 380 **sing another tune**	**態度[考え]を変える** ≒ change one's attitude [feeling]
□ 381 **sleep on it**	**一晩寝て考える** ≒ wait until tomorrow [later]
□ 382 **take the words right out of one's mouth**	**言おうとしていることを先に言う** ≒ say what another thinks
□ 383 **throw the book at ～**	**～をできるだけ厳しく罰する** ≒ give the maximum penalty to ～
□ 384 **upset the applecart**	**計画を台無しにする**、(問題を起こして)場[雰囲気]をめちゃくちゃにする ≒ completely spoil one's plan; disrupt the event [atomosphere]

You look as if you haven't gotten a wink of sleep in a week. You shouldn't spend so much time in the lab.	まるで１週間一睡もしなかったみたいに見えるよ。研究室でそんなに長い時間を過ごすべきじゃない。
I'd better get out and pound the pavement. Without a part-time job I'll never be able to make ends meet.	私は、外に出て仕事を探し回った方がいい。アルバイトなしでは絶対に生計を立てられないだろう。
I'm afraid my lab supervisor is really going to rake me over the coals when I tell her I haven't finished my experiment yet.	実験がまだ終わっていないと言ったら、私の研究室の指導教官は雷を落とすだろう。
Irene would sing another tune if she knew how her roommate really felt about her.	アイリーンは、ルームメートが自分のことを本当はどう思っているかを知ったら、態度を変えるだろう。
I think you should sleep on it before you decide to submit a report which is so critical of the current administration.	現経営陣にとても批判的な報告書の提出を決断する前に、一晩寝て考えた方がいいと思います。
You took the words right out of my mouth when you said Professor Lacy's a tough grader.	レーシー教授は評点が辛い人だ、と僕が言おうとしていたのに、君に先に言われちゃった。
The dean threw the book at Ned for copying his neighbor's paper during final exams; he's going to be expelled from school.	ネッドが期末テスト時に隣の人の答案を写したことについて、学部長は厳しく罰した。彼は退学させられるだろう。
Marty always seems to upset the applecart when you involve him in something fun.	君が何か楽しいことにマーティーを呼ぶと、彼はいつもそれを台無しにしてしまうようだ。

CD-A25

□385 **get a grasp of ～**	**～を理解する**、～をつかむ ≒ understand
□386 **get the better of ～**	**～に勝つ**、～を打ち負かす ≒ dominate
□387 **give ～ the thumbs down**	**～に反対する**、～を拒絶する ≒ reject; disapprove of ～
□388 **on the tip of one's tongue**	**口先まで出掛かって** ≒ almost remembered
□389 **once in a blue moon**	**非常にまれに** ≒ very rarely
□390 **the worse for wear**	〈人が〉**疲れ切って**、くたくたで ≒ in poor condition
□391 **wet behind the ears**	**青二才の**、未熟な ≒ inexperienced
□392 **a feather in one's cap**	**自慢の種**、誇りとなるもの ≒ a great achievement

continued ▼

If you don't get a grasp of the basics first, you'll never understand the more advanced stuff.

まず基礎を理解しなければ、より応用的なことなんて絶対にわからないだろう。

The chess master easily got the better of his inexperienced opponent.

そのチェスの名人は、未熟な相手をたやすく打ち負かした。

Too bad about Steve. I heard his advisor gave his research proposal the thumbs down.

スティーブは残念だったね。彼の指導教官は研究企画案に反対したそうだ。

Her name is right on the tip of my tongue, but I can't quite recall it.

彼女の名前が口先まで出掛かっているのに、いまひとつ出てこない。

John only plays his cello once in a blue moon.

ジョンは、非常にまれにチェロを弾く。

You look the worse for wear; did you have a busy weekend?

疲れ切ってるみたいだね。忙しい週末だったの？

Francine thinks she's ready to take on her own project, but the truth is that she's still wet behind the ears.

フランシーンは、いつでも独り立ちできると思っているが、実のところ彼女はまだ未熟である。

The scholarship that Lindsey was recently awarded is certainly a feather in her cap.

リンジーが最近受けた奨学金は、きっと自慢の種だ。

continued ▼

CD-A25(continued)

□393
a play-by-play account

詳細な説明[描写]
≒ a detailed description

□394
a whole new ballgame

新しい経験[出発]
≒ a fresh start; something completely different

□395
anybody's guess

予測できないこと、誰にもわからないこと
≒ not known by anyone

□396
It takes one to know one.

人のことばかり言えない。
• あなたが言っていることはあなた自身にも当てはまる、ということ。
≒ The same fault is present in the accuser.

□397
Old habits die hard.

古い習慣はなかなか直らないものだ。
≒ It's difficult to change one's behavior.

□398
Still waters run deep.

静かに流れる川は深い。
• 物静かな人は博識である、または激情を内に秘めている、ということ。
≒ Quiet people often think profoundly.

□399
There are more fish in the sea.

まだまだ機会はある。
≒ Other candidates are available.

□400
There's no accounting for taste.

たで食う虫も好き好き。
•人の好みはさまざまである、ということ。
≒ People can like strange things.

Get to the point, Mickey. I don't need a play-by-play account of every word that was said.	さっさと要点を言いなさい、ミッキー。すべての言葉についての細かい説明は要らないんだ。
This semester it'll be a whole new ball game. I'm going to attend every class and turn in every assignment on time.	今学期は新しい出発だ。私はすべての授業に出席し、すべての課題を期限通りに提出するつもりだ。
It's anybody's guess what type of questions will be on the final exam.	どんなタイプの問題が期末試験に出るのかわからない。
I suppose if I say that you're a workaholic you'll say that it takes one to know one.	私があなたを仕事中毒だと言ったら、あなたは自分のことを棚に上げて何言ってんのと言うでしょうね。

I thought Tim had turned over a new leaf, but old habits die hard, I suppose.	ティムは心を入れ替えたと思ったが、古い習慣はなかなか直らないようだ。
Don't let the fact that Joe's so quiet fool you. Still waters run deep; he's one of the smartest people I know.	ジョンがおとなしいやつだからってだまされちゃいけないよ。静かに流れる川は深いんだ。彼は僕が知っている人の中で最も頭が切れる一人だよ。
Sherman is despondent over losing his girlfriend, but he'll get over it as soon as he realizes how many more fish there are in the sea.	シャーマンはガールフレンドを失って落胆しているが、彼にはまだまだどれだけ多くの機会があるかを知ればすぐに乗り越えるだろう。
I never would've expected you to like country music. I guess there's just no accounting for taste.	君がカントリーミュージックを好きになるなんてこと、決して期待してなかった。人には好き好きがあると思うから。

復習テスト（Day 21-25）

（正解・訳例は pp.178-179）

1 赤字の意味としてもっともふさわしいものを A ～ D の中から選びなさい。

1. I know you're excited about the concert tonight, but try to contain yourself until then, will you?

A. 気持ちを抑える　B. 興奮を維持する　C. 思いを分かち合う　D. 思いの丈を語る

2. Outside opinions counted for nothing to the council.

A. 他に勝るとも劣らなかった　B. 他と比べようもないほど優れていた　C. 何の価値もなかった　D. 届くことはなかった

3. It's no use arguing with Michelle. She can dish it out, but she doesn't know how to take it very well.

A. 料理をする　B. 他人を非難する　C. 新しいことを思い付く　D. 大声でわめく

4. I was thinking about taking karate lessons, but I got cold feet when I saw how hard you have to train.

A. おじけづいた　B. 足が冷えた　C. 風邪を引いた　D. やる気になった

5. When I'm 30, I picture myself living in a quiet studio in France.

A. 自分の写真を撮る　B. 思い浮かべる　C. 肖像画を描く　D. 実行する

6. The officer made me pull over and asked for my driver's license and car registration.

A. 壁際に追い詰める B. 手を後ろに組む C. 車を脇に寄せる D. 両手を挙げる

7. They were supposed to deliver the product a week ago, and now no one is answering the phone. I smell a rat.

A. 腹が立つ B. 困惑する C. 警察に届ける D. 怪しく思う

8. The metal workers are threatening to walk out because of cutbacks at the plant.

A. 訴訟を起こす B. 調査をする C. 退職する D. ストライキをする

9. I don't know why, but every time I see Rudy he seems to give off unfriendly vibes toward me.

A. 払いのける B. 放つ C. 引き出す D. あきらめる

10. You should hang onto that old coin. I'm sure it's a collector's item.

A. 寄贈する B. 売り飛ばす C. 飾る D. 保持する

11. I feel sorry for Tom because people always poke fun at his southern accent.

A. 非難する B. 好む C. からかう D. 禁止する

12. Vandalism on the school campus should be ruthlessly stamped out.

A. 報告される	B. はびこる	C. 罰せられる	D. 撲滅される

13. I've spent all my money and have no one to go to for help. I'm in a real bind now.

A. 苦境にある	B. 保護を受けている	C. 嘆願中である	D. 拘束されている

14. Despite the fact that I spent most of my time preparing for the test, I got a C on it. It sure was a slap in the face for me.

A. 不意打ち	B. やる気	C. 侮辱	D. けじめ

15. I think O'Malley is giving you a real snow job. He's always pulling someone's leg.

A. 親切にしてくれている	B. 口先だけの話をしている	C. 援助してくれている	D. 割の合わない仕事を頼んでいる

16. "I hope my scholarship interview goes successfully. Wish me luck."
"Break a leg, Jim!"

A. 危ないよ	B. 思いっ切り行け	C. 幸運を祈ってるよ	D. 無謀だよ

17. I was so lost in thought that I didn't even notice when I missed my bus stop.

A. 物思いにふけっていた	B. 考えがまとまらなかった	C. 眠ってしまった	D. 考えることを放棄した

18. You look terrible this morning; why don't you call in sick and go to the doctor?

A. 病院で電話をする B. 病欠の連絡をする C. 病気がちだと伝える D. 病院の予約をする

19. I bought a really amazing new car last week. I feel like a million dollars.

A. 大金を使い後悔している B. お金をもっと稼げたらと思う C. 重荷になっている D. 最高の気分だ

20. I've never really liked Sally. The way she talks somehow gets under my skin.

A. 心に染みる B. 気に障る C. 風変りだ D. 落ち込ませる

21. I can't ask Matthew to do anything because he has his head in the clouds most of the time.

A. 集中している B. ぼんやりしている C. 有頂天になっている D. 居眠りしている

22. The recently imposed trade sanctions have given the oil companies a pretext for jacking up gas prices.

A. 価格をごまかす B. 価格を見直す C. 価格をつり上げる D. 価格交渉をする

23. George hid Patricia's glasses for a joke right before class and managed to keep a straight face while she was looking for them.

A. 熱心なふりをする B. 反省した表情をする C. 悲しそうにする D. 真顔でいる

24. I'm totally stressed out with my job. I definitely need to let my hair down.

A. 髪を切る B. 身支度を整える C. 考え直す D. 羽を伸ばす

25. "Even though my boss is very nice and helpful, I'm going to complain about him being late every day." "Don't bite the hand that feeds you, Sam."

A. 不満を言うな B. 遠慮するな C. 恩をあだで返すな D. 退職するな

26. I hear that there are still companies in the computer industry making money hand over fist.

A. 赤字を出している B. ぎりぎりの経営をしている C. ぼろもうけしている D. 若干黒字を出している

27. "You look pale today." "I was so nervous about the final exam that I couldn't get a wink of sleep last night."

A. 十分寝られた B. 一睡もできなかった C. 寝覚めが悪かった D. すぐに眠れなかった

28. I've got to pound the pavement for a new job because I can't find anything online.

A. 借金する B. 歩き回る C. 人に尋ねる D. 雑誌に目を通す

29. Clint agreed with my idea to change majors the other day but he sang another tune when I met him this morning.

A. 意見を変えた B. 反対のことを言った C. 話題を避けた D. 話をごまかした

30. "If you think it's too heavy a load for one semester, it's OK to drop some classes." "Well, let me sleep on it."

A. 一晩寝て考える B. 続ける C. 相談する D. いったん休む

31. "What a nasty and obnoxious professor!" "You took the words right out of my mouth."

A. それには賛成できない B. 話そうとしていたことを忘れた C. そう言おうとしていた D. そんなことを君が言うとは意外だ

32. Jeff upset the applecart by canceling the tour on the day we were supposed to leave.

A. 謝罪した B. 皆を落ち込ませた C. 計画を台無しにした D. 追い詰められた

33. I think I'm beginning to get a grasp of the math necessary for this problem.

A. 理解する B. 履修する C. 専攻する D. 敬遠する

34. When you're making a speech, don't let nervousness get the better of you. Just relax.

A. 勝つ B. 取り繕う C. 成長する D. 吸収する

35. "What did you think of the concert you went to last night?" "Well, I'm afraid I have to give it the thumbs down."

A. 駄目だ B. 称賛に値する C. 可もなく不可もない D. よくわからない

36. "Betty is a real complainer. I'm tired of it." "Let me say this, Daniel. It takes one to know one."

A. 確かにその通り	B. 人のことを言えない	C. 本音をぶつけるべき	D. そのうち好きになる

37. Even though he got married, Harry still can't keep his eye off other women. Old habits die hard, I guess.

A. 古い習慣はなかなかやめられない	B. 唯一の趣味なんだよ
C. そのうちあきれられるよ	D. 年を取っても遅すぎることはない

38. Richard usually stays silent during class, but when he talks everybody listens carefully. In his case, it really is true that still waters run deep.

A. 立て板に水	B. 静かに流れる川は深い	C. 世評に流されやすい	D. 備えあれば憂いなし

39. "Sherry gave me the cold shoulder and said she didn't want to see me anymore." "It's not such a big deal, Kyle. There are plenty more fish in the sea."

A. ほかのことを考えた方がいい	B. ほかにも女性はたくさんいる	C. あきらめるにはまだ早い	D. 時が解決してくれる

40. "I still don't get what Tony sees in a girl like Maria." "Well, there's no accounting for taste, I always say."

A. 人好き好きでしょう	B. 言っても無駄だよ	C. 金の力には勝てない	D. 人は見た目ではわからない

2 類義表現を a ～ j の中から選びなさい。

1. act up
2. come along
3. cut class
4. foot the bill
5. go off
6. kick the habit
7. take a dip
8. wait on ～

a. pay
b. digress
c. go swimming
d. skip a lesson
e. progress
f. serve
g. misbehave
h. dominate
i. fire
j. quit

---

9. null and void
10. on the blink
11. on the house
12. for a song
13. off the cuff
14. on second thought
15. on the tube
16. bread and butter

a. upon reconsidering
b. provided free
c. not legally binding; invalid
d. very cheaply
e. an insult
f. on television
g. not working properly
h. means of livelihood
i. a false story
j. without preparation; spontaneously

17. get in the way
18. get into a rut
19. get on one's nerves
20. get the cold shoulder
21. get the show on the road
22. have ants in one's pants
23. hear oneself think
24. put one's foot in one's mouth

a. have second thoughts; hesitate	b. say something inappropriate
c. follow the same dull routine	d. irritate one
e. concentrate (amid noise)	f. be treated indifferently
g. be restless; be impatient	h. begin
i. feel great	j. be an obstacle

---

25. be head and shoulders above ～
26. give ～ one's walking papers
27. go off the deep end with ～
28. have an ear for ～
29. make a clean breast of ～
30. meddle in ～
31. rake ～ over the coals
32. throw the book at ～

a. give the maximum penalty to ～	b. criticize ～ severely
c. eliminate ～ totally	d. give ～ liberally
e. get involved in ～	f. become obsessed with ～
g. fire; lay ～ off	h. be far better than ～
i. honestly account for ～	
j. have a natural understanding of ～	

33. on the tip of one's tongue
34. once in a blue moon
35. the worse for wear
36. wet behind the ears
37. a feather in one's cap
38. a play-by-play account
39. a whole new ballgame
40. anybody's guess

a. very cheeply
b. not known by anyone
c. be unrealistic [dreamy]
d. a fresh start; something completely different
e. a great achievement
f. in poor condition
g. very rarely
h. inexperienced
i. almost remembered
j. a detailed description

復習テスト（Day 21-25）正解・訳例

1

1. A	2. C	3. B	4. A	5. B	6. C	7. D	8. D	9. B	10. D
11. C	12. D	13. A	14. C	15. B	16. C	17. A	18. B	19. D	20. B
21. B	22. C	23. D	24. D	25. C	26. C	27. B	28. B	29. A	30. A
31. C	32. C	33. A	34. A	35. A	36. B	37. A	38. B	39. B	40. A

1. 君が今晩のコンサートでわくわくしてるのはわかるよ。でも、その時までは気持ちを抑える努力をしてはどうだい？
2. 審議会にとって、外部の意見など何の価値もなかった。
3. ミシェルと議論しても無駄よ。彼女、人を非難することはできても、（自分が非難された時には）どう我慢すればいいのか、よくわかってないもの。
4. 空手のレッスンを受けようかと思っていたんだけど、厳しい訓練が必要とわかって、おじけづいちゃったよ。
5. 30歳になった自分がフランスの静かなアトリエで暮らしてるところが目に浮かぶわ。
6. 警官は車を脇に寄せさせ、運転免許証と車検証を要求した。
7. その製品は1週間前に配達されるはずだったし、今は誰も電話に出ない。どうも怪しいな。
8. 金属工たちは、工場の縮小を理由にストライキを行うと脅しをかけている。
9. なぜだかわからないけど、ルディーに会うたびに、彼が私に対してよそよそしい雰囲気を発しているような気がするわ。
10. その古いコインは取っておくべきだな。きっと珍しいものだと思う。
11. 私は、トムについて気の毒に思っている。というのも、人々がいつも彼の南部なまりをからかっているからだ。
12. 大学構内での破壊行為は、容赦なく撲滅すべきだ。
13. お金をすっかり使い果たし、助けを求めに行ける人もいない。今本当に困ってるんだ。
14. ほとんどの時間をテストの準備に費やしたというのに、Cをもらった。僕に対する侮辱にほかならなかったよ。
15. オマリーは君をだましていると思うよ。彼はいつでも人をからかってばかりいるんだ。
16. 「奨学金の面接、うまくいくといいけど。僕の幸運を祈っててくれよ」「頑張れ、ジム！」
17. 私はすっかり物思いにふけっていたので、いつものバス停で降り損なったのにも気付かなかった。
18. けさは疲れてるようだね。電話で病欠するって連絡して、医者に行ったら？
19. 先週、本当にすごい新車を買ったんだ。最高の気分だよ。
20. サリーのことは、本当のところ好きじゃなかったんだ。彼女の話し方はなぜかこっちをいらいらさせる。
21. マシューには何も用事を頼めないわ。たいていは空想にふけっているんだもの。

22. 最近課された経済制裁は、石油会社にガソリンの価格を不正につり上げる口実を与えた。
23. ジョージは授業の直前にふざけてパトリシアの眼鏡を隠し、彼女が捜している間、澄ました顔をしていた。
24. 仕事のストレスで完全にへとへとよ。絶対に羽を伸ばす必要があるわ。
25. 「僕の上司はとてもいい人で力になってくれるけど、毎日の遅刻については苦情を申し立てるつもりだ」「恩をあだで返すのはやめなさいよ、サム」
26. コンピューター業界には、依然としてぼろもうけしている企業があると聞いている。
27. 「今日は、顔色が悪いよ」「最終試験のことですごく神経質になっちゃって、昨晩は一睡もできなかったの」
28. 新しい仕事を探して歩き回らなきゃ。インターネットでは何も見つからないんだから。
29. クリントは、専攻を変えるという僕の考えに先日は賛成したのに、けさ会ったら考えをがらりと変えていた。
30. 「1つの学期には負担が重過ぎると思うなら、授業の登録をいくつか取り消してもいい」「そうですね、一晩寝て考えさせてください」
31. 「なんていけ好かない、鼻持ちならない教授なんだろう！」「私もそう言おうと思ってたとこよ」
32. ジェフは、出発するはずだった日に旅行をキャンセルして、計画を台無しにした。
33. 僕は、この問題を解くのに必要な数学を理解し始めていると思う。
34. スピーチをするときは、緊張に負けてはいけない。とにかくリラックスすることだ。
35. 「君が昨晩行ったコンサートなんだけど、どうだった？」「うーん、残念だけど良くなかったって言わないと駄目かな」
36. 「ベティはとんでもない不平屋だね。もううんざりだよ」「言わせてもらうとね、ダニエル。人のことばかり言えないんじゃない」
37. ハリーは結婚したのに、ほかの女性からまだ目を離せずにいる。古い習慣って、なかなか直らないんだね。
38. リチャードは授業中たいていは静かにしているが、彼が口を開くと、皆が注意深く聞いている。彼の場合、静かに流れる川は深い、というのはまさに真実だね。
39. 「シェリーに冷たく当たられるし、彼女は僕にもう会いたくないんだって」「カイル、そんなの大したことじゃないさ。まだまだ機会はたくさんあるんだ」
40. 「トニーがマリアみたいな女の子のどこが気に入ってるのか、いまだにわからないよ」「うーん、たで食う虫も好き好きよ、いつも言ってるでしょ」

2

1. g	2. e	3. d	4. a	5. b	6. j	7. c	8. f	9. c	10. g
11. b	12. d	13. j	14. a	15. f	16. h	17. j	18. c	19. d	20. f
21. h	22. g	23. e	24. b	25. h	26. g	27. f	28. j	29. i	30. e
31. b	32. a	33. i	34. g	35. f	36. h	37. e	38. j	39. d	40. b

Chapter 4

チャレンジドリル 100

1 空所補充問題

CDを聞いて空所を埋めなさい。また、文の意味を考えなさい。
（正解・訳例は pp.196-200）

CD-B1

1. W: You made it back to the apartment 20 minutes ago? How'd you get back so fast?
M: Oh, I (　　　) (　) (　　　　) behind the auditorium.

2. M: But, Dr. Brunson, if you don't approve my topic now, all the time I've spent researching the paper will go (　　　) (　　) (　　　).
W: That's why I told everyone to see me before they started working on their papers.

3. M: Phil told me he got the job offer he was waiting for.
W: That's wonderful. He's probably (　　) (　　　) (　　　) right now.

4. W: What did Professor Buford say when you told him you hadn't completed your final paper?
M: He said it was (　　) (　　) (　　　) and I could take Composition 101 again in the spring.

5. M: I think Jeff took my lecture notes out of my briefcase.
W: You're (　　　　) (　　) (　　) (　　　　) (　　　). Jeff would never do that; somebody else must have taken them.

6. M: Are you almost done with your chemistry research?
W: Yes, thanks to Professor Anderson, who (　　　) (　　　) (　　　　　) to give us extra time in the lab.

7. W: Conrad hardly looked at a book all term and he ended up with a B average.
M: That's just like him to (　　　) (　　) (　　　　　) (　　) (　) (　　　).

8. M: With a new director, I should get a promotion in no time at all.
W: I wouldn't ( ) ( ) ( ) ( ) ( ) ( ).

9. M: I just can't seem to ( ) ( ) ( ) ( ) ( ) ( ) this semester.
W: Me, neither. I wish I were still on vacation.

10. W: David almost bit my head off when I told him I lost the book he lent me.
M: Oh, he always ( ) ( ) ( ) ( ) like that. By tomorrow he'll have forgotten all about it.

CD-B2

11. M: Half the time it seems like Carrie ignores me when I talk to her.
W: I've noticed the same thing. Most of what I say ( ) ( ) ( ) ( ) ( ) ( ) ( ) ( ).

12. M: Professor Snider proofread your whole thesis the day you gave it to him?
W: Yes. He's as busy as everyone else, but he ( ) ( ) ( ) ( ) ( ).

13. M: You've ( ) ( ) ( ) ( ) ( ) ( ) all day, Sarah.
W: Yes, the vice president wants this report in his hands by six.

14. M: What's your impression of the new housing director?
W: Terrific. She's the kind of woman who ( ) ( ) ( ) ( ) and gets the job done.

15. W: The new psychology labs are extraordinary.
M: Yes, they must have ( ) the school ( ) ( ) ( ) ( ) ( ).

16. M: Loise may have to drop out of school because she can't pay tuition.
W: I heard. Apparently her father's business has (　　　) (　　　) (　　　) (　　　).

17. M: I enjoyed listening to Pam's speech.
W: Me, too. She definitely (　　　) (　　) (　　　) (　　　) (　　　), that's for sure.

18. M: Sorry to interrupt you. I hope you didn't (　　　) (　　　) (　　　) (　　) (　　　).
W: As a matter of fact, I did. What was I saying?

19. M: Three months at this job and I still feel I haven't even (　　　) (　　　) (　　　) of what I need to know.
W: Don't worry, Thomas. In another month or two you'll start to have more confidence.

20. W: As your advisor, I have to be honest. Your scholarship application (　　　) (　　　) (　　　) (　　　) it: low grades and poor test scores.
M: Fortunately, two of my professors wrote glowing letters of recommendation. Maybe that'll be enough to save the day.

CD-B3

21. W: I don't understand it. My roommate's gone to bed before midnight three nights in a row.
M: Don't be so pessimistic, Karen. Maybe she's (　　　) (　　　) (　　) (　　　) (　　　).

22. W: I'm sorry I couldn't go to your piano recital. Something came up.
M: What it really (　　　) (　　　) (　　), Mary, is you only think about yourself.

23. M: Jack thinks he can keep on paying his rent late.
W: I'm afraid he's going to (　　　) (　　　) (　　　) (　　　) (　　　) that he can't keep doing that. The landlord told me she's going to evict him from his apartment.

24. M: Marsha told me Terry got kicked out of school.
W: It seems he was copying test answers from another student, and the professor (   ) him (   ).

25. M: The housing office just told me I never sent in my room application for next fall.
W: Oh no. (   ) (   ) (   ) (   ) (   ). I didn't either.

26. W: Well, what is it? A quiet coffee shop or the university library?
M: As far as getting my reading done, it's really (   ) (   ) (   ) (   ) (   ) (   ) (   ) (   ) (   ) (   ).

27. M: I heard they cut the budget for the women's track team.
W: You know how it is. Women's sports always get (   ) (   ) (   ) (   ) (   ) (   ).

28. W: I was able to sign up for Professor Larson's Biology 150, but unfortunately I couldn't get into Professor Barclay's Physics 250.
M: Just think of it as (   ) (   ) (   ) (   ) (   ) (   ) (   ). Those are two of the most popular teachers at the school.

29. W: Are you sure you can't go to the film festival this weekend?
M: (   ) (   ) (   ), Rebecca, (   ) that I need to study.

30. M: How long did they say it would take to fix the muffler?
W: They're so (   ) (   ) (   ) (   ) in repairs that they wouldn't promise anything until next week.

CD-B4

31. M: Have you talked to the new football coach? He seems like a real winner.
W: Don't (   ) (   ) (   ) (   ) (   ) (   ), Derek. Let's wait until the team plays some games before we decide that.

32. W: I told you I was in a hurry. Aren't our sandwiches ready yet?
M: (   ) (   ) (   ) (   ), lady. You're not the only customer, you know.

33. M: Have you really looked everywhere for that file?
W: Believe me, I've ( ) ( ) ( ) ( ). It's simply vanished into thin air.

34. W: Pam is more careful and precise in the lab than anyone I know.
M: She certainly ( ) ( ) ( ) ( ) ( ) ( ) ( ) a fine research chemist.

35. M: My boss forgot to pay me for the overtime I did last Saturday. I'm thinking about quitting and getting a different part-time job.
W: Don't ( ) ( ) ( ) ( ) ( ) ( ) ( ) ( ), Jack. I'm sure she can include it in your next paycheck.

36. M: Did you get the feeling that the sales representative was not being totally frank with us?
W: Well, he certainly didn't ( ) ( ) ( ) ( ) ( ) ( ) ( ) ( ), did he?

37. W: Do we really need to have the engine checked before this trip?
M: You bet. With all the driving ahead it's ( ) ( ) ( ) ( ) ( ) ( ).

38. W: I'll bet you're sitting ( ) ( ) ( ) ( ) waiting for the news about whether you got the scholarship or not.
M: That's the understatement of the year. I haven't had a good night's sleep in two weeks.

39. M: I'm really wondering whether I should go ahead and quit my job, then apply for one of the positions advertised in the newspaper.
W: Quit your job, Noah? Come on. ( ) ( ) ( ) ( ) ( ) ( ) ( ) ( ) ( ) ( ) ( ) ( ) ( ), especially in today's economy.

40. M: I'm so sorry to hear that you lost your job at the food service, Terri.
W: ( ) ( ) ( ) ( ) ( ) ( ) ( ). I really needed more time to study for finals, anyway.

CD-B5

41. M: Do you like the way our economics professor teaches?
W: Not at all. The way he nervously walks around in front of the class really ( ) ( ) ( ) ( ).

42. M: Katrina thinks she's going to get an A in biology.
W: She certainly ( ) ( ) ( ) ( ) ( ) ( ), doesn't she?

43. W: Ike has no idea how his words hurt other people, does he?
M: You can say that again. He's always ( ) ( ) ( ) ( ) ( ) ( ).

44. M: As a bookstore, Campus Text ( ) ( ) ( ) ( ) ( ) the Book Nook.
W: You can say that again. The Book Nook doesn't even carry magazines or newspapers.

45. M: My father is always bothering me about my grades. The next time he asks about them I'm going to blow a gasket.
W: I can understand telling him how you feel, but remember, he is paying your tuition, Jerry. Don't ( ) ( ) ( ) ( ) ( ) you.

46. M: Noah's really starting to ( ) ( ) ( ) ( ) ( ) ( ) his computer games.
W: You can say that again. He sits in his room all day and night staring at the computer screen.

47. W: How's Dennis doing these days? Is he still in publishing?
M: Yes. He owns his own company now, and from what I've heard he's ( ) ( ) ( ) ( ) ( ).

48. W: I'm wondering if I should complain to Professor Henry about all the work she's assigned us this term.
M: I wouldn't ( ) ( ) ( ), if I were you. She'll probably just hold it against you.

49. W: Do you remember the name of that Italian restaurant we had our New Year's party at?
M: Gee, it's (　　) (　　) (　　) (　　) (　　) (　　　　), but I can't quite remember it, either.

50. M: Johnnie is driving around in a pink Cadillac? You must be pulling my leg.
W: I'm not. (　　　　) (　　) (　　　　　　) (　　)
(　　　　), is there?

2 選択肢問題

CDを聞いて、設問の答えにふさわしいものを A ～ D の中から1つ選びなさい。（正解・スクリプト・訳例は pp.200-211）

CD-B6

1. □
A Withdraw some money.
B Order a cash card.
C Hand the man her identification.
D Close her savings account.

2. □
A Tom and his roommate fight a lot.
B Tom has yet to meet his roommate.
C Tom and his roommate get along well.
D Tom doesn't like his roommate.

3. □
A She's had enough already.
B She'd prefer a clean glass.
C She would like some lemonade.
D She has to leave soon.

4. □
A Shown her the materials first.
B Entered his model in the show.
C Cut out the design before beginning work.
D Constructed the model more carefully.

5. □
A She's been too busy to call.
B The dentist's schedule is full.
C She was not able to go to the dentist.
D The phone line's been busy.

6. □
A End the conflict with his roommate.
B Express his honest feelings.
C Avoid becoming violent.
D Admit his roommate was right.

7. □
A Stay away from gambling.
B Be satisfied with the vacation time she has.
C Bring back a present for her boss.
D Take a few extra days off next week.

8. ☐
A She doesn't like the two teams.
B She won't be able to attend the game.
C She was planning to purchase tickets.
D She was surprised the game was canceled.

9. ☐
A The woman should drop the course.
B He disagrees with her statement.
C The woman should attend class more often.
D He doesn't have time to talk right now.

10. ☐
A He's too busy to clean the room.
B He wants to delay cleaning the room.
C He thinks the room is quite clean.
D He feels the woman should help him.

CD-B7

11. ☐
A There is no charge for the roses.
B The woman should come back later.
C Roses are not available today.
D He'll prepare the flowers immediately.

12. ☐
A Professor O'Reilly's first name is Dean.
B His information is based on rumor.
C He prefers grape juice to wine.
D The announcement was made public.

13. ☐
A Take her to the sports gym.
B Spend the holidays with her mother.
C Go shopping for her mother's Christmas present.
D Visit home more frequently.

14. ☐
A She doesn't understand the man's question.
B She can't find her ticket to the game.
C She doesn't know what she'll do.
D She'll go home right after the game.

15. ☐
A She stopped at a grocery store.
B She doesn't like bacon.
C She often works late.
D She's supporting her family.

16. ☐

A He's not very friendly these days.
B He needs to work on his golf shot.
C They don't know him very well.
D He should have his shoulder checked by a doctor.

17. ☐

A The woman has not been doing well in school.
B He didn't know the woman was planning to come.
C The woman should apply for financial assistance.
D He would like to come over to visit.

18. ☐

A He's an honest person.
B He has very little chance of being elected.
C He speaks his mind directly.
D He avoids taking a clear position.

19. ☐

A Mr. Campbell has gone on a fishing trip.
B Mr. Campbell was fired from his job.
C Mr. Campbell is flying home from vacation.
D Mr. Campbell decided to pursue other challenges.

20. ☐

A The woman enjoys listening to music.
B The woman is very thoughtful.
C He doesn't want to be late for the performance.
D He hopes he can pay the woman back.

CD-B8

21. ☐

A She is not interested in going out with him later.
B He should repeat what he just said.
C The weather is not bad at all.
D He has no reason to be angry with her.

22. ☐

A When she plans to enter school.
B Whether she can be persuaded to continue.
C Whether she spoke with the woman recently.
D What plans she has after graduation.

23. ☐

A She agrees with what the man said.
B She would like to hit Linda.
C She thinks the man is exaggerating.
D She thinks the man is good with a hammer.

24. ☐
A His behavior was inappropriate.
B She doesn't have a good impression of him.
C She hasn't met him yet.
D He mistakenly moved into the wrong office.

25. ☐
A He's going on a diet soon.
B He doesn't believe his bag is too heavy.
C He's not as strong as he used to be.
D He wishes the woman wouldn't tease him.

26. ☐
A He hasn't had the job very long.
B He injured himself working.
C He doesn't like typing.
D He is not suited to his job.

27. ☐
A She basically agrees with the man.
B She thinks there are better professors than Dr. Donaldson.
C She feels that department is excellent.
D She considers Dr. Donaldson to be the brightest teacher.

28. ☐
A He's planning to drop out of school.
B Bertha should reduce her salt intake.
C He has no intention of leaving school.
D Bertha is taking classes in nutrition.

29. ☐
A He didn't like the professor's course.
B He's worried about his health.
C He's not interested in becoming a carpenter.
D He feels the course should be more lively.

30. ☐
A She often plays her music too loud.
B She frequently gets angry with her roommate.
C She has poor taste in footwear.
D She bought the wrong-sized shoes.

CD-B9

31.
- A Why the man wants hot water.
- B What the man plans to do next.
- C Why the man is in trouble.
- D What she can do to help the man.

32.
- A They are standing in a hay field.
- B The lights in the car need to be replaced.
- C It will be difficult to find the keys.
- D He should help look for her car.

33.
- A They drive quickly.
- B It isn't a big problem.
- C She'd like to take a vacation.
- D Ralph wants to buy a new car.

34.
- A He's nervous about the performance.
- B He has collected a lot of butterflies.
- C He has been feeling ill with the stomach flu.
- D He's not sure what he should play.

35.
- A She plans to speak as little as possible.
- B She hopes that she'll play the music well.
- C She's going to rehearse her answers in advance.
- D She'll do whatever seems right at the time.

36.
- A She probably didn't care much for camping.
- B She didn't really laugh that much.
- C She wasn't planning to take a walk.
- D She wasn't a very practical person.

37.
- A The company is planning to start a ranch.
- B The boss himself gave her the information.
- C She has just finished feeding the horses.
- D Her boss talks too much.

38.
- A He wants Lynn to go out dancing with him.
- B He believes the trouble is also his and Lynn's fault.
- C He suggests that Lynn should speak to the Ralstons.
- D He thinks the problem will get worse before it gets better.

39.

A She's worried too many people may come.
B She'd hoped the party would be more fun.
C The man's friends are welcome to attend.
D Her party is mainly for couples only.

40.

A The cost will be very high.
B The department will pay the lab charge.
C The school is upset at the high bill.
D The woman is in the wrong department.

CD-B10

41.

A Sailing.
B Playing tennis.
C Swimming.
D Eating ice cream.

42.

A It seems rather difficult.
B She shouldn't worry about it too much.
C Things will be better tomorrow.
D He thought this might happen.

43.

A He is not very organized.
B His eyes are bothering him.
C His computer is broken.
D He has an assignment due.

44.

A The talk wasn't prepared in advance.
B The talk wasn't very thorough.
C The professor was dressed too informally.
D The professor is getting over his cold.

45.

A She's happy she was accepted.
B The scholarship was even larger than she'd hoped for.
C She already mentioned it to Mark once before.
D The graduate program will be expensive.

46.

A He should be careful where he sits.
B His zoology experiment is almost finished.
C He's looking impatient.
D He wasn't paying attention to her.

47. ☐

A He said the same thing a moment ago.
B He forgot what he was going to say.
C He'd like the woman to repeat what she said.
D He agrees with the woman.

48. ☐

A Discuss a recent theater production.
B Play back a tape recording of the meeting.
C Pay his account in full.
D Describe the gathering in detail.

49. ☐

A It forces her to take a different way home.
B She hasn't heard how it's progressing.
C No one really knows when it will be finished.
D It should be completed in the fall.

50. ☐

A She should get to know Randy better.
B She has the same faults as Randy.
C Her new boss will be much kinder.
D Her opinion is usually quite valuable.

正解・訳例

（Check ▶ 000）の3けたの数字は、Chapter 1～3で学んだ見出しイディオムの通し番号を表します。間違えた人は、該当のイディオムを参照して復習しておきましょう。

1 （pp.182-188）

1. **took a shortcut** （Check ▶ 063）

【訳】
女：20分前にアパートに戻ったですって？　どうやってそんなに速く帰れたの？
男：ああ、講堂の裏を近道したんだ。
【語注】
make it to ～：～にたどり着く

2. **down the drain** （Check ▶ 102）

【訳】
男：ですがブランソン先生、もし今トピックを承認してくださらないと、この論文のリサーチに費やした時間すべてが無駄になってしまいます。
女：だから私は皆に、論文に取り掛かり始める前に私に会いに来るようにって言ったのよ。

3. **on cloud nine** （Check ▶ 117）

【訳】
男：待っていた仕事の口がもらえたって、フィルが言ってたよ。
女：それは良かったわ。彼、今ごろきっと有頂天だわね。

4. **the last straw** （Check ▶ 125）

【訳】
女：最終論文が仕上がってないってあなたが話したら、バフォード教授は何て言ったの？
男：我慢の限界だ、春にもう一度作文101を取れ、だって。
【語注】
Composition 101：アメリカやカナダの大学ではコース名の後に3けたの番号が付いていることが多い。通常、番号が若いほど初級レベルの内容である。

5. **barking up the wrong tree** （Check ▶ 129）

【訳】
男：僕のブリーフケースから講義メモを取ったのはジェフだと思うんだ。
女：それは見当違いよ。ジェフは絶対そんなことしない。取ったのはほかの人に違いないわ。

6. **bent over backwards** （Check ▶ 131）

【訳】
男：化学の研究はほとんど終わったの？
女：ええ、アンダーソン教授が、私たちに研究室で居残りする時間を与えようと全力を尽くしてくれたおかげでね。

7. **come out smelling like a rose** （Check ▶ 134）

【訳】
女：コンラッドは学期中ろくに本を見もしなかったのに、平均Bの成績だったのよ。
男：うまく切り抜けるところが彼らしいよ。

8. **count your chickens before they're hatched** （Check ▶ 135）

【訳】
男：新しい部長が来たら、僕はたちまち昇進するはずだ。
女：私なら、捕らぬたぬきの皮算用はしないわね。

9. **get into the swing of things** （Check ▶ 139）

【訳】
男：今学期はどうも調子が出ないなあ。
女：私もよ。まだ休暇中だったらいいのに。

10. **flies off the handle** （Check ▶ 146）

【訳】
女：デービッドに、彼から借りた本をなくしたって言ったら、怒鳴られかけたわ。
男：ああ、彼はいつもそんなふうにかっとなるんだ。明日にはけろっと忘れてるさ。
【語注】
bite one's head off：～を怒鳴りつける、～に食って掛かる

11. **goes in one ear and out the other** （Check ▶ 149）

【訳】
男：キャリーに話し掛けても、しょっちゅう無視される気がする。
女：私も同じことに気付いてたわ。私の言うことのほとんどが聞き流されちゃうの。
【語注】
half the time：しょっちゅう。「半分の時間は」か

ら転じて、この意味になった。

12. has a heart of gold (Check ▶ 150)

【訳】
男：スナイダー教授は、君が卒論を提出した日に全部読んでくれたのかい？
女：ええ。教授は、誰にも劣らず忙しいのに、思いやりがあるのよ。
【語注】
proofread：校正する。ここでは「(論文に)目を通す」の意で用いられている。

13. kept your nose to the grindstone (Check ▶ 151)

【訳】
男：君は一日中あくせく働いてるね、サラ。
女：ええ、副社長がこの報告書を6時までに欲しがってるの。

14. rolls up her sleeves (Check ▶ 158)

【訳】
男：新しいハウジング・ディレクターの印象はどう？
女：素晴らしいわ。腕まくりをして取り掛かってきっちり仕事をやるってタイプの女性ね。
【語注】
housing director：大学内の housing office では、寮、ホームステイなど、学生の住居に関して相談に乗ってくれる。

15. cost / an arm and a leg (Check ▶ 162)

【訳】
女：新しい心理学実験室、それはもうすごいのよ。
男：ああ、学校にとってはかなりの支出になったに違いないよ。

16. fallen on hard times (Check ▶ 164)

【訳】
男：ルイーズは、授業料が払えなくて、中退しなければならないかもしれないんだ。
女：聞いたわ。どうやらお父さんの事業が財政難に陥ったらしいわね。

17. has a way with words (Check ▶ 167)

【訳】
男：パムのスピーチを聞いて楽しかったよ。
女：私も。彼女は間違いなく話し上手ね、それは確かよ。

18. lose your train of thought (Check ▶ 170)

【訳】
男：話の腰を折ってごめん。言おうとしてたこと忘れてないといいけど。
女：実は忘れちゃったの。何の話をしてたかしら？

19. scratched the surface (Check ▶ 173)

【訳】
男：この仕事に就いて3カ月ですが、いまだに知るべきことを一通りなぞってさえいない気がします。
女：大丈夫よ、トーマス。もう1、2カ月もすれば、もっと自信が付いてくるでしょう。

20. has two strikes against (Check ▶ 182)

【訳】
女：指導教官として、正直にならないとね。あなたの奨学金申請書は不利な状況にあるの。成績も悪いし、テストの点もお粗末だから。
男：幸い、お世話になっている教授のうちのお2人が、熱の込もった推薦状を書いてくださいました。たぶんそれで十分うまくいくでしょう。
【語注】
glowing：熱の込もった、熱烈な
letters of recommendation：推薦状
save the day：土壇場で勝利をもたらす、急場を救う

21. turned over a new leaf (Check ▶ 192)

【訳】
女：理解できないわ。私のルームメート、3日連続で12時前に寝ちゃったのよ。
男：そう悲観するなよ、カレン。たぶん彼女は心を入れ替えたのさ。
【語注】
in a row：連続して

22. boils down to (Check ▶ 194)

【訳】
女：あなたのピアノリサイタルに行けなくてごめんなさい。用事ができちゃって。
男：メアリー、結局のところ、君は自分のことしか考えてないんだね。
【語注】
Something came up.：用事ができた。

23. **find out the hard way** （Check ▸ 197）
【訳】
男：ジャックは、家賃の支払いを遅らせ続けられると思ってるね。
女：残念だけど、そんなことを続けることはできないって、身をもって学ぶ羽目になるわね。大家さんが、彼をアパートから立ち退かせるつもりだって言ってたわ。
【語注】
evict A from B：A を B から立ち退かせる

24. **caught / red-handed** （Check ▸ 210）
【訳】
男：マーシャが言ってたけど、テリーが退学処分になったって。
女：テストでほかの学生の解答を写していて、その場で教授に見つかったらしいわ。
【語注】
get kicked out of school：退学処分になる

25. **Come to think of it** （Check ▸ 218）
【訳】
男：来秋の部屋の申請書を提出していないって、ハウジング・オフィスから言われたよ。
女：まあ。考えてみたら、私も提出してなかったわ。

26. **six of one and half a dozen of the other** （Check ▸ 220）
【訳】
女：ねえ、どうする？　静かなコーヒーショップ、それとも、大学の図書館？
男：読書を終わらせることにかけちゃ、実際のところ五十歩百歩だなあ。
【語注】
What is it?：どうする？

27. **the short end of the stick** （Check ▸ 221）
【訳】
男：女子の陸上競技チームの予算が削られたって聞いたよ。
女：知ってるでしょ。女子スポーツはいつも不利な扱いを受けるのよ。
【語注】
track team：陸上競技チーム。「陸上競技」は track and field。

28. **half a loaf is better than none** （Check ▸ 222）
【訳】
女：ラーソン教授の生物 150 には登録できたけど、残念ながらバークレー教授の物理 250 には入れなかったわ。
男：何も取れないよりましだと思えよ。学校で一番人気のある先生のうちの 2 人なんだから。

29. **The bottom line / is** （Check ▸ 224）
【訳】
女：今週末、映画祭に行けないって本当？
男：レベッカ、要するに、僕は勉強しなきゃならないんだよ。

30. **up to their necks** （Check ▸ 230）
【訳】
男：車のマフラーを修理するのにどれくらいの期間がかかるって言ってた？
女：たくさんの修理で身動きが取れないから、来週までは何とも言えないって。

31. **judge a book by its cover** （Check ▸ 282）
【訳】
男：フットボールの新しいコーチと話した？　すごいやり手みたいだよ。
女：見掛けで判断しないで、デレク。チームが何試合かこなすのを待ってから、判断しましょうよ。

32. **Keep your shirt on** （Check ▸ 284）
【訳】
女：急いでるって言ったでしょ。サンドイッチ、まだできないの？
男：落ち着いてください。お客さまはあなたお一人じゃないんですよ。

33. **left no stone unturned** （Check ▸ 285）
【訳】
男：そのファイルだけど、本当にあらゆる場所を捜したの？
女：本当よ、徹底的にやったわ。ただ跡形もなく消えうせちゃったの。
【語注】
vanish into the thin air：跡形もなく消えうせる。直訳すると「消えて希薄な空気になってしまう」。

34. **has what it takes to be** （Check ▸ 295）
【訳】
女：パムは、研究室では私が知っている誰よりも注意深くて正確よ。
男：彼女は、確かに優れた化学者になる器を備えているね。

35. make a mountain out of a molehill
(Check ▸ 297)

【訳】
男：僕が先週土曜にやった残業分の支払いを、上司が忘れたんだ。辞めて、別のアルバイトをやろうかな。
女：ささいなことを大げさに考えないでよ、ジャック。きっと次の給料に含めてくれるわ。

36. put all his cards on the table
(Check ▸ 300)

【訳】
男：あの営業担当者、僕たちに対してあんまり素直な態度で接していないって気がしなかった？
女：そうね、手の内を見せなかったことは確かよね？
【語注】
sales representative：営業担当者

37. better to be safe than sorry
(Check ▸ 305)

【訳】
女：この旅行の前に、本当にエンジンを点検してもらう必要があるの？
男：もちろん。これからずっと運転するんだから、転ばぬ先のつえってこと。

38. on pins and needles
(Check ▸ 309)

【訳】
女：奨学金がもらえたかどうかの連絡待ちで、きっとそわそわしているんでしょ。
男：そわそわどころじゃないよ。この2週間、一度もぐっすり眠れてないんだ。
【語注】
the understatement of the year：控えめ過ぎる言い方。～ of the year は、「とびきりの～」。

39. A bird in the hand is worth two in the bush (Check ▸ 315)

【訳】
男：思い切って仕事を辞めて、新聞に載ってた求人広告に応募した方がいいかなあ。
女：仕事を辞めるですって、ノア？ よしてよ。明日の百より今日の五十よ、特に今の経済情勢では。
【語注】
go ahead and do：思い切って～する

40. Every cloud has a silver lining
(Check ▸ 316)

【訳】
男：フードサービスの仕事を失ったんだってね、お気の毒さま、テリ。
女：苦は楽の種よ。どっちみち、期末試験の勉強をする時間がもっと必要だったの。

41. gets under my skin (Check ▸ 361)

【訳】
男：経済学の教授の教え方、気に入ってる？
女：全然。教室の前を神経質に歩き回られると、本当にいらいらするわ。

42. has her head in the clouds
(Check ▸ 363)

【訳】
男：カトリーナは、自分が生物でAを取るだろうと思ってるんだ。
女：間違いなく、空想の世界に行ってるわよね？

43. putting his foot in his mouth
(Check ▸ 368)

【訳】
女：アイクって、自分の言葉が他人をどう傷つけるか、全然わかってないわよね？
男：まったくだよ。まずいことばかり言っている。

44. is head and shoulders above
(Check ▸ 369)

【訳】
男：書店としては、キャンパス・テキストがブック・ヌックよりはるかに優れているね。
女：その通りだわ。ブック・ヌックには、雑誌や新聞さえ置いてないんだもの。

45. bite the hand that feeds
(Check ▸ 370)

【訳】
男：父はいつも成績のことで僕にうるさく言うんだ。今度成績について聞かれたら、ぶち切れてやる。
女：自分の気持ちを伝えるというのは理解できるけど、いい？ お父さんは学費を払ってくれているのよ、ジェリー。恩をあだで返すようなことはしないで。

46. go off the deep end with
(Check ▸ 372)

【訳】
男：ノアは、本当にコンピューターゲームにはまりかけてるよ。
女：その通りね。昼夜を問わず、ずっと部屋の中で、コンピューターの画面をにらんでるわ。

47. making money hand over fist
(Check ▸ 375)

【訳】
女：デニスはこのごろどう？　まだ出版業に携わっているの？
男：ああ。彼は、今じゃ自分の会社を所有してて、聞いたところでは、ぼろもうけしているって。

48. upset the applecart　(Check ▸ 384)

【訳】
女：今学期にあんなに課題を出されたことで、ヘンリー教授に苦情を言うべきかしら。
男：僕なら、波風を立てたりはしないな。たぶん、君のことをよく思わないだろう。
【語注】
hold A against B：A のことで B（人）を悪く思う

49. on the tip of my tongue　(Check ▸ 388)

【訳】
女：新年会を開いたイタリア料理店の名前、覚えてる？
男：うーん、口先まで出掛かってるんだけど、僕もはっきりとは思い出せないよ。

50. There's no accounting for taste
(Check ▸ 400)

【訳】
男：ジョニーがピンクのキャデラックを乗り回してるって？　僕をかついでるんだろ。
女：そんなことないわ。たで食う虫も好き好きでしょ？

2　(pp.189-195)

1. B

【スクリプト・訳】
M: Would you like a cash card for your passbook savings account, ma'am?
W: Hmm. That might come in handy.
Q: What will the woman probably do?
男：お客さまの通帳式普通預金口座に、キャッシュカードをお作りになりませんか。
女：うーん。ひょっとしたら役に立つかもしれないわね。
問：女性はおそらく何をするでしょうか。
【選択肢訳】
A お金をいくらか引き出す。
B キャッシュカードを注文する。
C 男性に身分証明書を手渡す。
D 預金口座を閉じる。
【解説】
「ひょっとしたら役に立つかもしれないわね」と女性。ここからこの後キャッシュカードを作ろうとすると推測される。passbook（預金通帳）、savings account（普通預金口座）は銀行でよく用いられる表現。
(Check ▸ 009 / come in handy)

2. C

【スクリプト・訳】
W: How does Tom like his new roommate?
M: They've really hit it off.
Q: What does the man imply?
女：トムは新しいルームメートをどう思ってるの？
男：2 人はすごく意気投合してたよ。
問：男性は何と言っていますか。
【選択肢訳】
A トムとルームメートはしょっちゅうけんかをする。
B トムはまだルームメートに会っていない。
C トムとルームメートはうまくやっている。
D トムはルームメートのことが好きではない。
【解説】
hit it off（仲良くなる、意気投合する）の意味がわかれば、正解は C だと判断できる。
(Check ▸ 012 / hit it off)

3. C

【スクリプト・訳】
M: Some lemonade, Meredith?
W: That would really hit the spot.

Q: What does the woman mean?
男：レモネードはどう、メレディス？
女：それに限るわね。
問：女性はどんなことを言っていますか。
【選択肢訳】
A もう十分飲んだ。
B きれいなグラスの方がよい。
C レモネードが飲みたい。
D すぐに出発しなくてはならない。
【解説】
「レモネードはどう、メレディス？」と男性。女性の発言にある hit the spot は「(飲食物が) 必要を満足させる、申し分ない」という意味で、ここではつまり、レモネードを飲みたいということである。
(Check ▶ 013 / hit the spot)

4. D

【スクリプト・訳】
M: If I'd only taken more time and used better materials, I'm sure my model airplane would've been the best in the show.
W: That's what happens when you try to cut corners.
Q: What does the woman imply the man should have done?
男：もっと時間をかけてもっといい材料を使いさえしていたら、きっと僕の模型飛行機がショーで一番だったろうに。
女：手を抜こうとすると、そういうことになるのよ。
問：女性は、男性がどうすべきだったと言っていますか。
【選択肢訳】
A 彼女に最初に材料を見せるべきだった。
B 自分が作った模型をショーに出品すべきだった。
C 作業を始める前にデザインを切り抜いておくべきだった。
D もっと注意深く模型を作るべきだった。
【解説】
cut corners は「角をきちんと通らず斜めに通る」ということから「(規則や安全性を無視して) 安易な方法でことを行う、手っ取り早いやり方をする」という意味で使われるようになった。ここでは「手を抜こうとすると、そういうことになるのよ」と女性。つまり、男性はもっと注意深く模型飛行機を作るべきだったということ。
(Check ▶ 018 / cut corners)

5. D

【スクリプト・訳】
M: Were you able to make an appointment for me at the dentist?
W: I still haven't gotten through.
Q: What does the woman mean?
男：僕の歯医者の予約、取れた？
女：まだ電話が通じないのよ。
問：女性は何と言っていますか。
【選択肢訳】
A 忙し過ぎて電話できなかった。
B 歯医者のスケジュールがいっぱいだ。
C 歯医者に行けなかった。
D 電話回線が込んでいた。
【解説】
「まだ電話が通じないのよ」と女性。電話回線が込んでいるためだ。
(Check ▶ 025 / get through [to ～])

6. A

【スクリプト・訳】
M: Since our fight, my roommate is still not talking to me.
W: Why don't you two just bury the hatchet?
Q: What does the woman suggest the man should do?
男：けんかして以来、ルームメートがいまだに口をきいてくれないんだ。
女：2人とも仲直りしたらどう？
問：女性は、男性がどうすべきだと言っていますか。
【選択肢訳】
A ルームメートとのけんかをやめる。
B 自分の正直な気持ちを話す。
C 暴力的にならないようにする。
D ルームメートが正しいことを認める。
【解説】
bury the hatchet (仲直りする) がわかれば正解はAだと判断できる。この表現は、ネイティブ・アメリカンが和解するとおの (hatchet) を土の中に埋めていた (bury) ことに由来している。
(Check ▶ 033 / bury the hatchet)

7. B

【スクリプト・訳】
W: My boss agreed to let me take off this week. Do you think I could get her to let me have a few days off next week, too?
M: If I were you, I wouldn't try to push my luck.
Q: What does the man suggest the woman should do?
女：上司が、今週の間休みを取らせてくれたの。来週も何日か取らせてもらえると思う？
男：僕だったら、欲張らないけどな。
問：男性は、女性がどうすべきだと言っていますか。
【選択肢訳】
A ギャンブルには手を出さない。
B 今もらっている休暇で満足する。
C 上司にプレゼントを持ち帰る。
D 来週もう何日か休暇を取る。
【解説】
男性のアドバイスは何か。「上司が、今週の間休みを取らせてくれたの。来週も何日か取らせてもらえると思う？」と女性。「僕だったら、欲張らないけどな」と男性。つまり「もらえた休暇分で満足しなさい」と言いたいのだ。
(Check ▶ 046 / push one's luck)

8. D
【スクリプト・訳】
M: Did you hear that the game got called off?
W: Are you kidding me?
Q: What does the woman imply?
男：試合が中止になったって聞いた？
女：冗談でしょ？
問：女性は何と言っていますか。
【選択肢訳】
A その2チームが好きではない。
B 試合には参加できないだろう。
C チケットを買うつもりだった。
D 試合が中止になって驚いた。
【解説】
女性の発言から何がわかるか。Are you kidding me?（冗談でしょ？）から、驚いていることがわかるはず。
(Check ▶ 065 / call off ～)

9. B
【スクリプト・訳】
W: I'm not sure if I can handle advanced calculus.
M: Cut it out, Michelle.
Q: What does the man mean?
女：上級微積分学のクラスでうまくやっていけるか、自信がないわ。
男：よせよ、ミシェル。
問：男性は何と言っていますか。
【選択肢訳】
A 女性はそのクラスを辞めるべきである。
B 彼女の発言に異議がある。
C 女性はもっと頻繁に授業に出席すべきである。
D 今話をしている時間がない。
【解説】
「上級微積分学のクラスでうまくやっていけるか、自信がないわ」と女性。「よせよ、ミシェル」と男性。文脈からB「彼女の発言に異議がある」が正解となる。クラスを辞めるべきだという話ではないので、Aは間違い。
(Check ▶ 070 / cut out ～)

10. B
【スクリプト・訳】
W: Phil, you really need to clean your dorm room.
M: Oh, I can put it off a bit longer, can't I?
Q: What does the man imply?
女：フィル、あなた本当に寮の部屋を掃除しなきゃ。
男：ああ、もうちょっと後回しにしてもいいだろ？
問：男性は何と言っていますか。
【選択肢訳】
A 忙し過ぎて部屋の掃除ができない。
B 部屋の掃除を先延ばしにしたい。
C 部屋はかなりきれいだと思う。
D 女性が手伝うべきだと感じている。
【解説】
I can put it off a bit longer, can't I?（もうちょっと後回しにしてもいいだろ？）と男性。put off ～は、2問前に出てきたcall off ～とともに押さえておきたい表現だ。
(Check ▶ 078 / put off ～)

11. D
【スクリプト・訳】
W: Are the dozen roses I ordered ready?
M: I'll have them for you in nothing flat.
Q: What does the man mean?
女：注文した1ダースのバラは用意できていますか。
男：今すぐお持ちいたします。
問：男性は何と言っていますか。
【選択肢訳】
A バラは無料だ。
B 女性は後で戻ってくるべきだ。
C 今日はバラが手に入らない。
D その花をすぐに用意する。
【解説】
in nothing flat が聞き取りのポイント。Dではこれがimmediatelyに言い換えられている点に注意。
(Check ▶ 115 / in nothing flat)

12. B

【スクリプト・訳】

W: Are you sure that Professor O'Reilly will be named dean?
M: That's what I heard through the grapevine.
Q: What does the man mean?
女：オライリー教授が学部長に任命されるって確かなの？
男：人づてにはそう聞いたけど。
問：男性は何と言っていますか。

【選択肢訳】

A オライリー教授の名前はディーンだ。
B 自分の情報はうわさに基づいている。
C 自分はワインよりぶどうジュースのほうが好きだ。
D その発表が公になされた。

【解説】

grapevine は「ぶどうのつる」で、くねくねしているところから「いろいろな人の口を伝わって」というニュアンス。「人づてにそう聞いたけど」とはつまり B「自分の情報はうわさ（rumor）に基づいている」ということ。
（Check ▶ 119 / through the grapevine）

13. B

【スクリプト・訳】

M: We went to your mother's last year for Christmas.
W: Come on, Jim, be a good sport. She only gets to see us once a year.
Q: What does the woman want the man to do?
男：君のお母さんの家には去年のクリスマスに行ったよね。
女：お願い、ジム、自分本位にならないでよ。母は1年に1回しか私たちに会えないんだから。
問：女性は男性にどうしてほしいのですか。

【選択肢訳】

A 自分をスポーツジムに連れて行く。
B 休暇を自分の母親と一緒に過ごす。
C 自分の母親へのクリスマスプレゼントを買いに行く。
D もっと頻繁に家を訪問する。

【解説】

「君のお母さんの家には去年のクリスマスに行ったよね」と男性。「自分本位にならないでよ。母は1年に1回しか私たちに会えないんだから」と女性。つまり、B「休暇を自分の母親と一緒に過ごす」ことを望んでいるのだ。
（Check ▶ 121 / a good sport）

14. C

【スクリプト・訳】

M: What do you plan to do after the homecoming game, Jackie?
W: Search me.
Q: What does the woman mean?
男：大学祭の試合の後は何をするつもり、ジャッキー？
女：わからないわ。
問：女性は何と言っていますか。

【選択肢訳】

A 男性の質問が理解できない。
B 試合のチケットが見つからない。
C 何をするかわからない。
D 試合の後すぐ家に帰るだろう。

【解説】

Search me. = I have no idea. のことだとわかれば正解は C だと判断できる。
（Check ▶ 128 / Search me.）

15. D

【スクリプト・訳】

M: This is the third night in a row you've worked late.
W: Well, someone has to bring home the bacon.
Q: What does the woman mean?
男：君の残業は、これで三夜連続になるね。
女：まあ、誰かが生活費を稼がなくっちゃね。
問：女性は何と言っていますか。

【選択肢訳】

A 食料品店に立ち寄った。
B ベーコンは好きではない。
C しょっちゅう残業する。
D 自分が家族を養っている。

【解説】

bring home the bacon（家にベーコンを持ち帰る）は、伝統的にボーリング大会の賞品に豚が使われていたことから「(家族を養うだけの)生活費を稼ぐ」の意になっている。
（Check ▶ 132 / bring home the bacon）

16. A

【スクリプト・訳】

M: What's going on with David recently?
W: I don't know. He sure seems to have a chip on his shoulder, though, doesn't he?
Q: What do the people say about David?
男：デービッドは最近どうしてる？
女：さあね。けんか腰なのは確かなようだけど、でしょ？
問：2人はデービッドについて何と言っていますか。
【選択肢訳】
A 彼はこのごろあまり好意的ではない。
B 彼はゴルフのショットを練習する必要がある。
C 彼のことをあまりよく知らない。
D 彼は医者に肩を診てもらうべきだった。
【解説】
デービッドは最近どうなのか。「けんか腰なのは確かなようだけど」と女性。つまりA「彼はこのごろあまり好意的ではない」のだ。選択肢を柔軟にとらえることも大切だ。
(Check ▶ 142 / have a chip on one's shoulder)

17. A
【スクリプト・訳】
W: The dean said I might lose my scholarship next semester.
M: Well, with grades like yours, Sherry, I guess you have it coming.
Q: What does the man imply?
女：私、来学期は奨学金をもらえなくなるかもしれないって、学部長に言われたわ。
男：うーん、シェリー、君のような成績じゃ自業自得だね。
問：男性は何と言っていますか。
【選択肢訳】
A 女性は学業が振るわなかった。
B 自分は、女性が来るつもりなのを知らなかった。
C 女性は金銭的援助を求めるべきだ。
D 自分は訪ねて来たいと思う。
【解説】
scholarshipとは「奨学金」のこと。男性の「君のような成績じゃ自業自得だね」とはつまりA「女性は学業が振るわなかった」のだ。
(Check ▶ 143 / have it coming)

18. D
【スクリプト・訳】
W: Are you going to vote for Frank for class president?
M: If I knew what he stood for. He's always beating around the bush.
Q: What does the man say about Frank?
女：学級委員長には、フランクへ投票するつもり？
男：彼が何を支持してるのか、わかればね。彼はいつも回りくどいんだ。
問：男性はフランクについて何と言っていますか。
【選択肢訳】
A 彼は正直な人だ。
B 彼が選ばれる見込みはほとんどない。
C 彼は自分の考えを率直に話す。
D 彼は態度をはっきりさせることを避ける。
【解説】
「彼が何を支持してるのか、わかればね。彼はいつも回りくどいんだ」と男性。つまり遠回しではっきりしないと言いたいのだ。
(Check ▶ 161 / beat around the bush)

19. D
【スクリプト・訳】
W: Do you mean Mr. Campbell is no longer with the company?
M: That's right. I guess he had other fish to fry.
Q: What does the man mean?
女：キャンベル氏がもう会社を辞めたって言うの？
男：そうだよ。ほかにやるべきことがあったんじゃないかな。
問：男性は何と言っていますか。
【選択肢訳】
A キャンベル氏は釣り旅行に行ってしまった。
B キャンベル氏は仕事を首になった。
C キャンベル氏は休暇から飛行機で帰ってくる。
D キャンベル氏は別の目標を追求することにした。
【解説】
女性の発言が聞き取りのポイント。have other fish to fry（ほかに揚げる魚がある）とは、高温の油で魚を揚げている最中は、人に呼ばれても目を離さず、そちらを優先しなければならないことから、「ほかに大事な用事［やるべきこと］がある」という意味で使われるようになった。
(Check ▶ 168 / have other fish to fry)

20. B
【スクリプト・訳】
W: Since your parents will be in town this weekend, I got tickets for the dinner theater.
M: You certainly don't miss a beat, Sylvia, do you?
Q: What does the man mean?
女：今週末はご両親が街にいらっしゃるから、ディナー・シアターのチケットを買ったわ。
男：君は本当に気が利くね、シルビア。
問：男性は何と言っていますか。
【選択肢訳】
A 女性は音楽鑑賞が大好きだ。
B 女性は大変気配りができる。
C ショーに遅れたくない。

D 女性にお返しができたらいいと思う。
【解説】
You certainly don't miss a beat. が聞き取りのポイント。don't miss a beat とは「拍子を外さない」ということで、転じて「(いつもとは違う状況であっても) とまどわない、ちゅうちょしない、まごつかない」ということ。ここでは thoughtful (気配りができる) が一番近いので B が正解。
(Check ▶ 171 / not miss a beat)

21. D
【スクリプト・訳】
M: You're simply not listening to anything I say tonight.
W: Richard, if you've had a bad day, please don't take it out on me.
Q: What does the woman suggest to the man?
男：君は単に、今夜の僕の話を一言も聞いていないんだな。
女：リチャード、嫌な1日だったからって、私に八つ当たりしないで。
問：女性は男性に何と言っていますか。
【選択肢訳】
A 後で彼と外出することには興味がない。
B 彼は今言ったことを繰り返すべきだ。
C 天気は全然悪くない。
D 彼が女性に対して怒る理由はない。
【解説】
「嫌な1日だったからって、私に八つ当たりしないで」と女性。つまり、男性が女性を怒る理由は何もないということ。
(Check ▶ 174 / take out A on B)

22. B
【スクリプト・訳】
W: Patty told me that she's pretty much decided to drop out of school this term.
M: That would be terrible. Do you think we can talk her out of it?
Q: What does the man want to know about Patty?
女：パティーが、今学期で中退することをほぼ決めたって言ってたわ。
男：そりゃまずいな。僕らで中退しないように説得できると思う？
問：男性はパティーについてどんなことを知りたいのですか。
【選択肢訳】
A 彼女がいつ入学するつもりか。
B 彼女が (学校を) 続けるように説得できるかどうか。
C 彼女が最近 (今、男性と話している) 女性と話したかどうか。
D 卒業後、彼女がどんな計画を持っているか。
【解説】
drop out of school は「中退する」の意。男性はパティーについて何が知りたいのか。説得して退学をやめさせることができるかどうかである。
(Check ▶ 176 / talk A out of B)

23. A
【スクリプト・訳】
M: The problem with Linda is that she's so selfish.
W: You certainly hit the nail right on the head.
Q: What does the woman mean?
男：リンダについて問題なのは、彼女がひどくわがままだってことだよ。
女：まさに図星だわ。
問：女性は何と言っていますか。
【選択肢訳】
A 男性が言ったことに賛成だ。
B リンダを殴りたい。
C 男性の言うことは大げさだと思う。
D 男性はハンマーを扱うのがうまいと思う。
【解説】
「まさに図星だわ」と女性。男性の意見に同意しているのである。
(Check ▶ 184 / hit the nail on the head)

24. B
【スクリプト・訳】
M: What do you think of our new counselor?
W: Oh, I don't know. Something about him rubs me the wrong way.
Q: What does the woman imply about the new counselor?
男：新しいカウンセラーのこと、どう思う？
女：どうかしらね。彼には、私の神経を逆なでするところがあるわ。
問：女性は新しいカウンセラーについて何と言っていますか。
【選択肢訳】
A 彼の行動は不適切だった。
B 彼についていい印象を持っていない。
C まだ彼に会っていない。
D 彼は間違って違うオフィスに移ってしまった。
【解説】
女性は新しいカウンセラーをどう思っているのか。

Something about him rubs me the wrong way. が聞き取りのポイント。あまりよく思っていないのだ。
(Check ▶ 188 / rub ～ the wrong way)

25. D
【スクリプト・訳】
W: Putting on a little weight, aren't you, Danny?
M: Yeah, but you don't have to rub it in.
Q: What does the man mean?
女：少し太ったでしょ、ダニー？
男：ああ、でもわざわざ言うことないだろ。
問：男性は何と言っていますか。
【選択肢訳】
A すぐにダイエットを始めるつもりだ。
B 自分のバッグが重過ぎるとは思わない。
C 自分は以前ほど強くない。
D 女性に、からかってほしくないと思う。
【解説】
rub it in がわからないと正解を選べない。「わざわざ言うことないだろ」と男性が言っているので、D が正解。put on [gain] weight は「太る」。
(Check ▶ 189 / rub in ～)

26. D
【スクリプト・訳】
W: Why the long face?
M: I just don't think I'm cut out for this type of work.
Q: What does the man mean?
女：どうして仏頂面をしているの？
男：僕はこの手の仕事には向いてないと思うんだ。
問：男性は何と言っていますか。
【選択肢訳】
A この仕事をそれほど長くやっていない。
B 仕事中にけがをした。
C キーボード入力は好きではない。
D 自分の仕事に向いていない。
【解説】
the long face とは「仏頂面」のこと。がっかりしたときの「寂しそうな顔」の場合にも用いられる。ちなみに「仏頂面をする」は put on [make] a long face と言う。
(Check ▶ 193 / be cut out for ～)

27. B
【スクリプト・訳】
M: I think Dr. Donaldson is by far the best teacher in the department, don't you?
W: He can't hold a candle to some of the other faculty.
Q: What does the woman mean?
男：ドナルドソン先生は学部内で断然一番の先生だと思うよ、そう思わない？
女：ほかの何人かの先生には及ばないわ。
問：女性は何と言っていますか。
【選択肢訳】
A 基本的には男性に賛成である。
B ドナルドソン先生より優れた教授がいると思う。
C その学部は優秀だと思う。
D ドナルドソン先生が一番聡明な先生だと思う。
【解説】
「ほかの何人かの先生には及ばないわ」と女性。つまり B「ドナルドソン先生より優れた教授がいると思う」が正解。
(Check ▶ 195 / can't hold a candle to ～)

28. C
【スクリプト・訳】
W: Bertha told me that you were thinking of dropping out of school.
M: I'd take everything Bertha says with a grain of salt.
Q: What does the man imply?
女：あなたが中退を考えてる、ってバーサに聞いたけど。
男：僕なら、バーサの言うことはすべて話半分で聞くね。
問：男性は何と言っていますか。
【選択肢訳】
A 学校を中退するつもりである。
B バーサは塩分摂取量を減らすべきだ。
C 退学の意思はない。
D バーサは栄養学の授業を取っている。
【解説】
「あなたが中退を考えてる、ってバーサに聞いたけど」と女性。「僕なら、バーサの言うことはすべて話半分で聞くね」と男性。つまり C「退学の意思はない」ことが推測できる。
(Check ▶ 201 / take ～ with a grain of salt)

29. A
【スクリプト・訳】
W: Are you going to take another class from Professor Carpenter?
M: Over my dead body I will!
Q: What does the man imply?
女：カーペンター教授の授業をもう一つ取るつも

り？
男：絶対取らないよ！
問：男性は何と言っていますか。
【選択肢訳】
A その教授の講座は好きではなかった。
B 自分の健康が心配だ。
C 大工になることには興味がない。
D その講座はもっと活発であるべきだ。
【解説】
Over my dead body は「自分が生きているうちは、絶対にない（させない）」ということ。提案や陳述に強い反対の意を表すときに用いる。ここでは「カーペンター教授の授業は絶対取りたくない」という意味。従って A「その教授の講座は好きではなかった」ことがわかる。
（Check ▸ 233 / over my dead body）

30. B
【スクリプト・訳】
W: My roommate got angry at me for playing my music too loud last night.
M: So the shoe is on the other foot now, is it?
Q: What does the man imply about the woman?
女：昨晩、私のかける音楽がうるさ過ぎるって、ルームメートに怒られたわ。
男：ということは、今回は立場が逆転したってわけだね？
問：男性は女性について何と言っていますか。
【選択肢訳】
A しばしばうるさい音量で音楽をかける。
B ルームメートに対して頻繁に怒る。
C 履物の趣味が悪い。
D 間違ったサイズの靴を買った。
【解説】
the shoe is on the other foot の意味がわからなければ正解を選べない。「今回は立場が逆転したってわけだね」ということだから、いつもは彼女の方がルームメートに対して怒っているのである。
（Check ▸ 238 / The shoe is on the other foot.）

31. C
【スクリプト・訳】
M: I'm really in hot water, now.
W: Why, what happened?
Q: What does the woman want to know?
男：今すごく困ってるんだ。
女：まあ、何があったの？
問：女性は何を知りたいのですか。
【選択肢訳】
A 男性が湯を欲しがっている理由。
B 男性が次にやろうとしていること。
C 男性が困っている理由。
D 男性を助けるために自分ができること。
【解説】
in hot water が in trouble と同じ意味だとわかれば、正解は C だとすぐに判断できる。
（Check ▸ 264 / in hot water）

32. C
【スクリプト・訳】
M: Is this where you think you dropped the keys?
W: Yeah, but in the dark it'll be like looking for a needle in a haystack.
Q: What does the woman imply?
男：鍵を落としたと思う場所はここかい？
女：ええ、でも、暗い中じゃ、見つけるのは至難の業ね。
問：女性は何と言っていますか。
【選択肢訳】
A 2 人は干し草用の畑に立っている。
B 車のライトを取り替える必要がある。
C 鍵を捜すのは難しいだろう。
D 自分の車を捜すのを男性が手伝うべきだ。
【解説】
女性の「干し草の山の中から針 1 本を捜すようなものだ」とは、見つけるのは至難の業だということ。文字どおりに考えてもピンとくるイディオムだ。
（Check ▸ 273 / be like looking for a needle in a haystack）

33. B
【スクリプト・訳】
M: How do you and Ralph manage with only one car?
W: Oh, we somehow get by.
Q: What does the woman mean?
男：たった 1 台の車で、君とラルフはどうやってやり繰りするの？
女：あら、何とかやっていくわ。
問：女性は何と言っていますか。
【選択肢訳】
A 2 人は車を速く走らせる。
B それは大した問題ではない。
C 休暇を取りたいと思う。
D ラルフは新しい車を買いたがっている。

【解説】
「何とかやっていくわ」と女性。つまりそんなに大きな問題ではないということ。
（Check ▶ 275 / get by）

34. A
【スクリプト・訳】
W: We're all looking forward to your senior concert next week, Bob.
M: Thanks, but I already have butterflies in my stomach.
Q: What does the man mean?
女：私たちみんな、来週のあなたの最終学年のコンサートを楽しみにしてるのよ、ボブ。
男：ありがとう、でも、僕はもう緊張してるんだ。
問：男性は何と言っていますか。
【選択肢訳】
A 演奏について、緊張している。
B 多くの蝶を収集してきた。
C ウイルス性胃腸炎で具合が悪かった。
D 何を演奏すべきかわからない。
【解説】
have butterflies in one's stomach = be nervous がわかればすぐ正解が導き出せる。「おなかに蝶々がいる」という直訳からも、緊張しているそのニュアンスをうかがえる。
（Check ▶ 280 / have butterflies in one's stomach）

35. D
【スクリプト・訳】
M: So what's your strategy for the job interview on Friday, Michelle?
W: I'm going to play it by ear as much as possible.
Q: What does the woman mean?
男：じゃあ、金曜の就職面接はどんな作戦で行くつもりだい、ミシェル？
女：なるべく臨機応変にやるつもりよ。
問：女性は何と言っていますか。
【選択肢訳】
A なるべく話さないつもりだ。
B 上手に音楽を演奏できればなあと思う。
C 答えを前もって練習するつもりだ。
D 何でも、その時にふさわしいと思われることをする。
【解説】
play it by ear の意味がわからなければ正解を得ることは難しい。「楽譜なしで耳だけを頼りに演奏する」から転じて「臨機応変にやる」の意になった表現だ。ad-lib も同じ意味で使える。
（Check ▶ 299 / play it by ear）

36. A
【スクリプト・訳】
W: I'm really looking forward to the hiking club's weekend camping trip.
M: No kidding? I just can't imagine you roughing it.
Q: What had the man assumed about the woman?
女：ハイキングクラブの週末のキャンプ旅行、本当に楽しみだわ。
男：冗談だろ？　君が自然のままの生活をするところなんて想像できないよ。
問：男性は女性についてどう思っていましたか。
【選択肢訳】
A おそらくキャンプがあまり好きではない。
B それほど笑わない。
C 散歩するつもりはない。
D あまり実務的な人間ではない。
【解説】
男性は女性のことをどう思っていたのか。「冗談だろ？　君が自然のままの生活をするところなんて想像できないよ」と述べている。つまり、たぶんキャンプには興味がないと思っていたのだ。
（Check ▶ 301 / rough it）

37. B
【スクリプト・訳】
M: You're sure the boss is thinking of opening a new branch office?
W: I got it straight from the horse's mouth.
Q: What does the woman mean?
男：上司が新しい支店を開くことを考えてるって確かかい？
女：本人から直接聞いたわ。
問：女性は何と言っていますか。
【選択肢訳】
A 会社は牧場を始めるつもりである。
B 上司自身がその情報を与えた。
C ちょうど馬にえさをやり終えたところだ。
D 上司はおしゃべりが過ぎる。
【解説】
そのものずばり straight from the horse's mouth がわかれば正解は B だと判断できる。上司自らが女性に話したのだ。このようなイディオムは知らないと何のことかさっぱりわからない。文脈とともに例文に触れて、使い方をマスターしよう。
(Check ▶ 311 / straight from the horse's mouth)

38. B

【スクリプト・訳】

W: The Ralstons are always fighting with us. They've got to be the most unreasonable neighbors we've ever had.
M: Come on, Lynn, it takes two to tango.
Q: What does the man mean?
女：ロールストン家とうちはいつもけんかばかり。あの一家は今までで一番聞き分けのない隣人だわ。
男：よせよ、リン、お互いさまだ。
問：男性は何と言っていますか。

【選択肢訳】

A リンに、一緒にダンスをしに出掛けてほしい。
B このトラブルは自分とリンにも非があると思う。
C リンがロールストン家と話すべきだと提案している。
D その問題はいったん悪化してから好転するだろうと思っている。

【解説】

unreasonable neighbors とは「聞き分けのない隣人」ということ。it takes two to tango は「タンゴを踊るには2人必要」ということで、「1人では問題は起きないはず、どちらにも非はある」という意味になる。Each side is to blame. や Both sides should be blamed. などともいえる。
(Check ▶ 317 / It takes two to tango.)

39. C

【スクリプト・訳】

M: Do you mind if I invite a couple of my friends to your party Saturday night?
W: The more the merrier, as far as I'm concerned.
Q: What does the woman mean?
男：土曜の晩のパーティーに僕の友人を2人招待してもいいかな？
女：私に言わせれば、人は多ければ多いほど楽しいわ。
問：女性は何と言っていますか。

【選択肢訳】

A 人が大勢来過ぎるかもしれないのが心配だ。
B パーティーがもっと楽しかったら良かったのに。
C 男性の友人の参加は歓迎だ。
D パーティーは主として夫婦連れに限る。

【解説】

「土曜の晩のパーティーに僕の友人を2人招待してもいいかな？」と男性。The more the merrier（人は多ければ多いほど楽しいわ）と女性。つまり歓迎しているのである。as far as I'm concerned（私に言わせれば、私に関する限り）は決まり文句。
(Check ▶ 320 / The more the merrier.)

40. B

【スクリプト・訳】

M: I bet the lab fees for this class will be really expensive.
W: Haven't you heard that the department is footing the bill?
Q: What does the woman mean?
男：このクラスの実験費、きっとかなりの額になるよ。
女：学部が支払ってくれるって、聞かなかった？
問：女性は何と言っていますか。

【選択肢訳】

A 費用はとても高額になるだろう。
B 学部が実験費を支払うだろう。
C 学校は高額の請求書に腹を立てている。
D 自分は間違った学部にいる。

【解説】

「このクラスの実験費、きっとかなりの額になるよ」と男性。「学部が支払ってくれるって、聞かなかった？」と女性。foot the bill = pay より B が正解。
(Check ▶ 327 / foot the bill)

41. C

【スクリプト・訳】

W: Ah, nothing like taking a dip after an afternoon of tennis.
M: You can say that again.
Q: What are the man and woman doing?
女：ああ、午後のテニスの後のひと泳ぎは格別ね。
男：まったくだよ。
問：男性と女性は何をしていますか。

【選択肢訳】

A ヨットを走らせている。
B テニスをしている。
C 泳いでいる。
D アイスクリームを食べている。

【解説】

この2人は何をしているのか。「午後のテニスの後のひと泳ぎは格別ね」と女性。テニスをしているのではない。take a dip（ひと泳ぎする）がわかれば、正解は C だと判断できる。
(Check ▶ 334 / take a dip)

42. A
【スクリプト・訳】
W: Oh no, I have two meetings both scheduled for 10 o'clock tomorrow.
M: Well, it looks like you're really in a bind.
Q: What does the man imply about the woman's situation?
女：やだ、2つのミーティング、両方とも明日の10時に入ってるわ。
男：うーん、だいぶ困った様子だね。
問：女性の状況について男性は何と言っていますか。
【選択肢訳】
A かなり難しそうだ。
B 彼女はそのことをあまり心配すべきではない。
C 明日には状況が好転するだろう。
D 自分は、そうなるかもしれないと思った。
【解説】
男性は女性の状況をどう見ているのか。you're really in a bind という発言から、困っていると判断しているのがわかる。
(Check ▶ 341 / in a bind)

43. C
【スクリプト・訳】
W: It's not often I see you in the computer lab, Rudy. What's up?
M: I have no choice. My own system is on the blink.
Q: What does the man mean?
女：ルディー、コンピューター室ではあまり会わないのに。どうしたの？
男：仕方ないんだ。僕のシステムが故障しちゃって。
問：男性はなんと言っていますか。
【選択肢訳】
A 自分はあまりまめではない。
B 目の具合が気になっている。
C 自分のコンピューターが故障している。
D 提出期限の来た課題を抱えている。
【解説】
on the blink = not working properly がわかれば正解は C だと判断できる。
(Check ▶ 343 / on the blink)

44. A
【スクリプト・訳】
W: Professor Carlson's talk to the student body was one of the best I've heard.
M: Would you believe it was totally off the cuff?
Q: What does the man mean?
女：学生自治会に対するカールソン教授の講演は今まで聞いた中でも最高だったわ。
男：あれが全くの即興だったなんて信じられる？
問：男性は何と言っていますか。
【選択肢訳】
A 講演は前もって準備したものではなかった。
B 講演はあまり綿密なものではなかった。
C 教授の服装はくだけ過ぎていた。
D 教授は風邪が治りかけだ。
【解説】
off the cuff が聞き取りのポイント。カールソン教授の話は、前もって準備されたものではなかったということである。the student body は「学生自治会」。
(Check ▶ 346 / off the cuff)

45. A
【スクリプト・訳】
M: I heard you got into the graduate program you applied to.
W: Yeah, and I tell you, Mark, I feel like a million dollars.
Q: What does the woman mean?
男：出願していた大学院課程に入学したんだって？
女：ええ、それでねえ、マーク、私、最高の気分なの。
問：女性は何と言っていますか。
【選択肢訳】
A 入学できて幸せだ。
B 奨学金は望んでいたよりもずっと高額だった。
C そのことは以前マークにすでに話した。
D 大学院課程はかなり費用がかさむだろう。
【解説】
I feel like a million dollars がポイント。女性は、大学院に合格して最高の気分なのだ。
(Check ▶ 355 / feel like a million dollars)

46. C
【スクリプト・訳】
W: What's wrong, Reggie? You look like you have ants in your pants.
M: Isn't this lecture ever going to end?
Q: What does the woman imply about the man?
女：どうかしたの、レジー？　そわそわしてるみたいだけど。
男：この講義、終わりそうにないね？
問：女性は男性について何と言っていますか。
【選択肢訳】
A 座る場所に気を付けるべきだ。

B 彼の動物学の実験はほとんど終わっている。
C 彼は待ち切れなくなっているように見える。
D 彼は女性に注意を払っていなかった。
【解説】
You look like you have ants in your pants（そわそわしているみたいだ）とは look impatient ということ。
(Check ▸ 362 / have ants in one's pants)

47. D
【スクリプト・訳】
W: This is one of the most beautiful days we've had so far this year.
M: You took the words right out of my mouth.
Q: What does the man mean?
女：今日は今年になって一番うららかな日ね。
男：僕もそう言おうと思ってたところだよ。
問：男性は何と言っていますか。
【選択肢訳】
A 今しがた自分も同じことを言った。
B 何を言おうとしていたか忘れた。
C 女性に、言ったことを繰り返してもらいたい。
D 自分も女性に賛成だ。
【解説】
You took the words right out of my mouth. とは、直訳すれば「口から出掛けた言葉を相手がすっと取ってしまった」で、「僕もそう言おうと思ってたところだよ」の意。従って、女性と同じことを考えていたのである。
(Check ▸ 382 / take the words right out of one's mouth)

48. D
【スクリプト・訳】
W: Do you know what happened at the student government meeting last night?
M: I can give you a play-by-play account, if you like.
Q: What will the man probably do?
女：昨晩、学生自治会の会合で何があったのか知ってる？
男：何なら、事細かに説明してあげるよ。
問：男性はおそらくどんなことをするでしょうか。
【選択肢訳】
A 最近の演劇作品を論ずる。
B 会合の録音テープを再生する。
C 自分の勘定を全額支払う。
D 会合のことを詳細に説明する。
【解説】
play-by-play は「詳細な」という意味の形容詞。従って、後ろには名詞が来ることに注意。
(Check ▸ 393 / a play-by-play account)

49. C
【スクリプト・訳】
M: Do you think they'll get the road construction done this summer?
W: As far as I know, it's anybody's guess.
Q: What does the woman imply about the road repair?
男：道路工事は今年の夏で終わると思う？
女：私の知る限り、誰にもわからないわね。
問：女性は道路工事について何と言っていますか。
【選択肢訳】
A 工事のために別の道で帰宅しなくてはならない。
B 進捗状況を聞いていない。
C いつ終わるのか、実際は誰も知らない。
D 工事は秋に終わるはずだ。
【解説】
「誰も推測しかできない」とはつまり、誰も知らないということ。get the road construction done で「道路工事を終わらせる」の意。これは、the road construction is done を get してくれる状態と考えるとわかりやすい。
(Check ▸ 395 / anybody's guess)

50. B
【スクリプト・訳】
W: Cathy keeps saying that Randy's a dictator.
M: Well, I guess it takes one to know one.
Q: What does the man imply about Cathy?
女：ランディーは独裁者だって、キャシーがいつも言っているわ。
男：うーん、人のことばかり言えないんじゃない。
問：男性はキャシーについて何と言っていますか。
【選択肢訳】
A ランディーのことをもっとよく知るべきだ。
B 彼女にはランディーと同じ欠点がある。
C 彼女の新しい上司はずっと寛大だろう。
D 彼女の意見はたいていの場合、とても貴重だ。
【解説】
it takes one to know one とは「人を批判するような人も同じような欠点があるもの」ということ。結局キャシーも dictator（独裁者）のようなところがあると言いたいのだ。
(Check ▸ 396 / It takes one to know one.)

INDEX

見出しイディオムは赤字、それ以外のものは黒字で示されています。右側にある数字は、そのイディオムが掲載されている見出しの番号を表しています。また、各ページの下には、意味がわかったイディオム表現の数の合計を書き込むためのチェックボックスを２回分用意してあります。習熟度の推移を測る目安としてお役立てください。

Index

A

B

どれだけチェックできた? 1 □ 2 □

☐ be told ~ directly	296	
☐ be treated indifferently	359	
☐ be unable to control oneself	276	
☐ be unexpectedly canceled	021	
☐ be unfamiliar	225	
☐ be unique	030	
☐ be unrealistic [dreamy]	363	
☐ **be up to ~**	**001**	
☐ be useful	009	
☐ be very expensive	162	
☐ be very hungry	136	
☐ be very kind	150	
☐ be visible [noticeable]	030	
☐ be what ~ deserves	215	
☐ be worth ~	324	
☐ **bear up**	**241**	
☐ **beat around the bush**	**161**	
☐ become clear	159	
☐ become furious	242	
☐ become happy	008	
☐ become obsessed with ~	372	
☐ become popular	034	
☐ become suddenly angry	146	
☐ become very angry	257	
☐ begin	042, 360	
☐ begin doing ~ promptly	294	
☐ begin over	148	
☐ begin to do	037	
☐ **bend over backwards**	**131**	
☐ **better (to be) safe than sorry**	**305**	
☐ **bite the hand that feeds ~**	**370**	
☐ blame ~ officially	291	
☐ **blow a gasket**	**242**	
☐ **blow up**	**002**	
☐ **boil down to ~**	**194**	
☐ **bread and butter**	**351**	
☐ break	003	
☐ **Break a leg.**	**352**	
☐ **break down**	**003**	
☐ break off discussions	336	
☐ **break the ice**	**177**	
☐ **break up**	**004**	
☐ briefly	108	
☐ **bring ~ down to earth**	**289**	
☐ **bring ~ up to date**	**290**	
☐ **bring home the bacon**	**132**	
☐ buried	230	
☐ **bury the hatchet**	**033**	

C

☐ **call ~ on the carpet**	**291**	
☐ **call in sick**	**354**	
☐ **call it a day**	**133**	
☐ **call off ~**	**065**	
☐ calm down	284	
☐ cancel	065	
☐ **can't complain**	**005**	
☐ **can't hold a candle to ~**	**195**	
☐ **can't make heads or[nor] tails of ~**	**197**	
☐ can't understand ~ at all	197	
☐ care for ~	087	
☐ **catch ~ red-handed**	**210**	
☐ catch <an illness>	053	
☐ **catch on**	**034**	
☐ **catch one's eye**	**006**	
☐ **catch up on ~**	**211**	
☐ cause ~ irritation	188	
☐ **cause a stir**	**007**	
☐ cause minor conflicts	044	
☐ **(the) chances are (that) ~**	**126**	
☐ change one's attitude [feeling]	380	
☐ change one's ways [habits]	192	
☐ **cheer up**	**008**	
☐ **chew out ~**	**066**	
☐ **chip in ~**	**052**	
☐ clumsy	227	
☐ **come along**	**322**	
☐ **come down with ~**	**053**	
☐ **come in handy**	**009**	
☐ **come out smelling like a rose**	**134**	
☐ **come to think of it**	**218**	
☐ **come up with ~**	**067**	
☐ complete	064	
☐ completely spoil one's plan	384	
☐ compromise	088	
☐ concentrate (amid noise)	364	
☐ concentrate on ~	214	
☐ conclude	004, 202	
☐ consider	200	
☐ consider a minor problem to be serious	297	
☐ contact someone to advise that one cannot work due to illness	354	
☐ **contain oneself**	**323**	
☐ contend with ~	092	
☐ continue with ~	261	
☐ contribute	052	
☐ control one's emotion	323	
☐ conversation	272	
☐ **cost ~ an arm and a leg**	**162**	
☐ **couldn't be better**	**017**	

☐ count for ~	324
☐ count on ~	068
☐ count out ~	081
☐ **count your chickens before they're hatched**	**135**
☐ crazy	229
☐ create	244
☐ create a controversy	007
☐ create a relaxed atmosphere	177
☐ criticize ~ severely	379
☐ criticize <a subordinate>	291
☐ **cut class**	**325**
☐ **cut corners**	**018**
☐ **cut down on ~**	**069**
☐ Cut it [that] out.	070
☐ **cut out ~**	**070**

D

☐ **day in and day out**	**204**
☐ defend	062, 260
☐ delay	014, 078, 250
☐ depend on ~	049
☐ depressed	306
☐ describe A as B	156
☐ deserve it	143
☐ design	244
☐ **die of hunger**	**136**
☐ digress	329
☐ **dirt cheap**	**263**
☐ disapprove of ~	387
☐ discover ~ first-hand	210
☐ discuss	075
☐ dish it out	326
☐ **dish out ~**	**326**
☐ dislike and want to harm ~	180
☐ disrupt the event [atmosphere]	384
☐ dissuade A from B	176
☐ divide the cost	047
☐ do more than one usually would	131
☐ dominate	386
☐ **down in the dumps**	**306**
☐ **down the drain**	**102**
☐ doze off	243
☐ **draw up ~**	**244**
☐ **drive at ~**	**245**
☐ **drop by ~**	**071**
☐ **drop in on ~**	**163**
☐ drop in to ~	071
☐ **drop off ~**	**082**, 076

E

☐ Each side is to blame.	317
☐ easier than expected	314
☐ eat a lot	137
☐ eat in a restaurant	019
☐ **eat like a horse**	**137**
☐ **eat out**	**019**
☐ either way is about the same	220
☐ eliminate ~ totally	340
☐ emerge from a bad situation successfully	134
☐ encounter	092
☐ encounter financial difficulties	164
☐ end	004
☐ **end up doing**	**010**
☐ endure	079
☐ escape responsibility	266
☐ eventually be successful	254
☐ eventually become ~	226
☐ eventually have to do	010
☐ **Every cloud has a silver lining.**	**316**
☐ every day	204
☐ exchange	099
☐ expect the best outcome	135
☐ extremely clean	268
☐ extremely happy	308

F

☐ fail the program	274
☐ fail to keep pace	028
☐ fail to keep up	020
☐ **fall behind**	**020**
☐ **fall on hard times**	**164**
☐ **fall through**	**021**
☐ fare	252
☐ feel great	355
☐ **feel like a million dollars**	**355**
☐ feel real	159
☐ feeling extremely happy	117
☐ **figure out ~**	**054**
☐ **fill A in on B**	**138**
☐ find	067
☐ find a middle ground	088
☐ **find out ~ the hard way**	**196**
☐ find time for ~	292
☐ find time to do	165
☐ finish it	140
☐ finish talking on the phone	147
☐ finish work for the day	133
☐ fire	371

☐ firsthand	311	
☐ **fit ~ in**	292	
☐ **fit as a fiddle**	307	
☐ **flunk out**	274	
☐ **fly off the handle**	146	
☐ follow the same dull routine	357	
☐ **food for thought**	271	
☐ **foot the bill**	327	
☐ **for a change**	106	
☐ for a long time	232	
☐ **for a song**	345	
☐ **for next to nothing**	231	
☐ **for nothing**	113	
☐ for sure	120	
☐ forget what one planned to say	170	
☐ forsake	304	
☐ **from scratch**	114	
☐ from the very beginning	114	
☐ **from time to time**	205	
☐ fullfill a small amount	173	

G

☐ **get ~ off one's chest**	293
☐ **get a grasp of ~**	385
☐ get a punctured tire	040
☐ **get ahold of ~**	083
☐ get along	252
☐ **get along (with ~)**	022
☐ **get an early start on ~**	294
☐ get angry	287
☐ **get around**	011
☐ **get around to doing**	165
☐ **get at ~**	072
☐ **get by**	275
☐ **get carried away**	276
☐ **get cold feet**	328
☐ **get in the way**	356
☐ **get into a rut**	357
☐ **get into the swing of things**	139
☐ get involved in ~	376
☐ **get it over with**	140
☐ **get lost**	023
☐ get married	255
☐ **get nowhere (with ~)**	024
☐ **get off the phone**	147
☐ **get on one's nerves**	358
☐ **get on the ball**	141
☐ **get one's own way**	277
☐ **get over ~**	073
☐ get over it	144
☐ **get the better of ~**	386

☐ **get the cold shoulder**	359
☐ **get the hang of ~**	212
☐ **get the lead out**	278
☐ **get the show on the road**	360
☐ **get through (to ~)**	025
☐ get to work	158
☐ **get together**	035
☐ **get under one's skin**	361
☐ **get under way**	246
☐ **get up on the wrong side of the bed**	279
☐ get up to date with ~	211
☐ get used to the situation	139
☐ **give ~ a hand**	074
☐ **give ~ a lift**	084
☐ give ~ a ride	084
☐ give ~ current information	290
☐ give ~ liberally	326
☐ **give ~ one's walking papers**	371
☐ **give ~ the thumbs down**	387
☐ **give credibility (to ~)**	036
☐ **give in**	026
☐ **give off ~**	337
☐ give the maximum penalty to ~	383
☐ **go ahead**	037
☐ go away	023
☐ **go back to square one**	148
☐ go back to the beginning	148
☐ **go Dutch**	038
☐ **go easy on ~**	085
☐ **go in for ~**	247
☐ **go in one ear and out the other**	149
☐ **go off**	329
☐ **go off the deep end with ~**	372
☐ go on strike	336
☐ **go out on a limb**	178
☐ **go over ~**	055
☐ **go overboard**	039
☐ go swimming	334
☐ go to bed	248
☐ go to extremes	039
☐ go too far	046
☐ Good luck!	352
☐ Good things also come from bad situations.	316
☐ gossip	272
☐ **grab a bite**	166
☐ gradually stop having an effect	256

H

☐ **Half a loaf is better than none.**	222

どれだけチェックできた？ 1 ☐ 2 ☐

☐ handle the load	241
☐ hang onto ~	338
☐ have a bad attitude	142
☐ have a chip on one's shoulder	142
☐ have a flat (tire)	040
☐ have a heart of gold	150
☐ have a lot on one's mind	179
☐ have a natural understanding of ~	373
☐ have a way with words	167
☐ have all been bought	051
☐ have an ear for ~	373
☐ have ants in one's pants	362
☐ have butterflies in one's stomach	280
☐ have fun without worrying about what others think	367
☐ have good relations (with ~)	022
☐ have it coming	143
☐ have it in for ~	180
☐ have it out	181
☐ have no more ~	091
☐ have no time available	130
☐ have one's feet on the ground	281
☐ have one's head in the clouds	363
☐ have other fish to fry	168
☐ have other interests	168
☐ have second thoughts	328
☐ have things how one wants them	277
☐ have two strikes against ~	182
☐ have what it takes to be ~	295
☐ Having a little of something is better than having nothing.	222
☐ healthy	307
☐ hear ~ firsthand	296
☐ hear oneself think	364
☐ help	074
☐ help oneself to ~	183
☐ hesitate	328
☐ hit it off	012
☐ hit the books	041
☐ hit the ceiling	257
☐ hit the hay	248
☐ hit the nail on the head	184
☐ hit the spot	013
☐ hold off	014
☐ hold one's horses	249
☐ hold up ~	250
☐ honestly account for ~	374
☐ hurry up	278

I

☐ I agree totally.	234

☐ I couldn't agree more.	234
☐ I don't feel the same as you.	237
☐ I have no idea.	128
☐ I won't do it!	235
☐ ignore	304
☐ imagine A to be B	156
☐ imagine oneself doing	331
☐ imply	072, 245
☐ in a bind	341
☐ in a difficult situation	341
☐ in a flash	107
☐ in a nutshell	108
☐ in ages	232
☐ in good condition	307
☐ in hot water	264
☐ in nothing flat	115
☐ in one piece	265
☐ in poor condition	390
☐ in seventh heaven	308
☐ in the dark	103
☐ in the nick of time	206
☐ in trouble	264
☐ in vain	113
☐ inaccurate	312
☐ inexperienced	391
☐ inform A of B	138
☐ instead of doing the usual thing	106
☐ invalid	342
☐ investigate thoroughly	285
☐ involuntarily fall asleep	243
☐ iron out ~	251
☐ irritate one	358, 361
☐ it is likely (that) ~	126
☐ It takes one to know one.	396
☐ It takes two to tango.	317
☐ It's certain.	239
☐ It's difficult to change one's behavior.	397

J

☐ jack up the price	365
☐ joke	045
☐ judge a book by its cover	282
☐ jump the gun	015
☐ just before time ran out	206

K

☐ keep	338
☐ keep a straight face	366
☐ keep clear of ~	056
☐ keep in touch	185
☐ keep on one's toes	283

☐ **keep one's nose to the grindstone**	151
☐ **keep one's shirt on**	284
☐ **keep to oneself**	027
☐ **keep track of ~**	152
☐ **keep up with ~**	186
☐ keep working hard	151
☐ **kick around ~**	075
☐ **kick off**	042
☐ **kick the habit**	330
☐ **knock it off**	043
☐ **knock oneself out**	169

L

☐ **lag behind**	028
☐ lay ~ off	371
☐ learn ~ through a bad experience	196
☐ learn how to do ~	212
☐ learn the basics	057
☐ **learn the ropes**	057
☐ **leave A up to B**	153
☐ **leave no stone unturned (doing)**	285
☐ leaving	267
☐ **let off ~**	076
☐ **let on that ~**	086
☐ **let one's hair down**	367
☐ let out ~	076
☐ **let the cat out of the bag**	286
☐ **let up**	154
☐ like to do ~	247
☐ **live up to ~**	077
☐ live without modern conveniences	301
☐ **look after ~**	087, 098
☐ **look high and low for ~**	213
☐ look in the wrong place	129
☐ lose control	287
☐ **lose one's head**	287
☐ lose one's temper	002
☐ **lose one's train of thought**	170
☐ **lose the thread**	155

M

☐ maintain a record of ~	152
☐ maintain contact	185
☐ maintain the same level with ~	186
☐ make ~ annoyed	188
☐ make ~ clear	093
☐ make ~ recognize reality	289
☐ **make a clean breast of ~**	374
☐ make a lot of money	375
☐ **make a mountain out of a molehill**	297

☐ **make A out to be B**	156
☐ make contact with ~	083
☐ **make ends meet**	157
☐ make genuine effort to find a job	378
☐ make good use of ~	097
☐ **make money hand over fist**	375
☐ **make no difference**	058
☐ make no progress (with ~)	024
☐ make one feel satisfied	013
☐ **make out**	252
☐ make room in the schedule for ~	292
☐ **make sense**	059
☐ make use of ~	262
☐ **make waves**	044
☐ manage	241
☐ means of livelihood	351
☐ **meddle in ~**	376
☐ meet	035
☐ meet ~ by accident	090
☐ **meet ~ halfway**	088
☐ meet one's standards	077
☐ misbehave	321
☐ misdirect anger about A toward B	174
☐ More people will be more fun.	320
☐ more than that	203
☐ move away from the main point	155
☐ move from one place to another	011

N

☐ never	233
☐ **no big deal**	122
☐ No denying it.	223
☐ **No doubt about it.**	223
☐ **no way**	109
☐ not a chance	109
☐ **Not again!**	127
☐ not an important issue	122
☐ not an option	207
☐ not be cruel to ~	085
☐ not follow the correct procedures	018
☐ **not get a wink of sleep**	377
☐ not include ~	081
☐ not known by anyone	395
☐ not legally binding	342
☐ **not miss a beat**	171
☐ **Not on your life!**	235
☐ **not ring a bell**	225
☐ not skilled	227
☐ not sleep at all	377
☐ not throw away	338
☐ not waste one's effort	288

どれだけチェックできた？ 1 ☐ 2 ☐

☐ not working properly	343
☐ **nothing short of ~**	104
☐ **(every) now and then**	116
☐ now that I consider it	218
☐ **null and void**	342

O

☐ occasionally	112, 205
☐ **off the cuff**	346
☐ **off the hook**	266
☐ official sanction	124
☐ officially start	089
☐ Oh no! Yet another time!	127
☐ **Old habits die hard.**	397
☐ **on and off**	110
☐ **on cloud nine**	117
☐ **on one's way out**	267
☐ **on pins and needles**	309
☐ **on second thought**	347
☐ **on short notice**	111
☐ on television	348
☐ **on the blink**	343
☐ **on the cutting edge**	228
☐ **on the dot**	269
☐ **on the house**	344
☐ **on the tip of one's tongue**	388
☐ **on the tube**	348
☐ **once in a blue moon**	389
☐ **(every) once in a while**	112, 116
☐ One sure thing is better than a possibility.	315
☐ **open up to ~**	253
☐ organize oneself	141
☐ Other candidates are available.	399
☐ **out of one's mind**	229
☐ **out of the blue**	310
☐ **out of the question**	207
☐ **over and over**	118
☐ **over my dead body**	233
☐ overloaded	230

P

☐ pay	327
☐ pay an unfair price	298
☐ pay equally	038
☐ pay for everything	172
☐ pay one's expenses	157
☐ **pay through the nose**	298
☐ People can like strange things.	400
☐ periodically	110
☐ pick up the bill	172
☐ **pick up the tab**	172
☐ **picture oneself doing**	331
☐ **play it by ear**	299
☐ **poke fun at ~**	339
☐ possess the capability to be ~	295
☐ postpone	078
☐ **pound the pavement**	378
☐ precisely at a certain time	269
☐ proceed	037
☐ progress	322
☐ **pros and cons**	123
☐ provided free	344
☐ publicize a secret	286
☐ **pull off ~**	187
☐ **pull one's leg**	045, 258
☐ **pull over**	332
☐ **pull through**	254
☐ **push one's luck**	046
☐ **put ~ into effect**	089
☐ **put ~ on**	258
☐ **put all one's cards on the table**	300
☐ put faith (in ~)	036
☐ **put off ~**	078
☐ **put one's foot in one's mouth**	368
☐ **put one's mind to ~**	214
☐ **put up with ~**	079

Q

☐ quickly get something to eat	166
☐ Quiet people often think profoundly.	398
☐ quit	330

R

☐ raise the price unfairly	365
☐ **raise the roof**	016
☐ **rake ~ over the coals**	379
☐ reach (~) by phone	025
☐ reach a conclusion based on appearance	282
☐ recover	254
☐ recover completely	145
☐ recover from ~	073
☐ reduce	069
☐ refrain from laughing	366
☐ register for ~	191
☐ reject	080, 387
☐ relax	031
☐ rely on ~	049
☐ rely upon ~	068
☐ rely upon B to do A	153
☐ remain awake	048

☐ remove	070
☐ repeatedly	118
☐ replace	099
☐ represent	324
☐ resolve	061, 251
☐ result in being ~	216
☐ reveal one's hidden thoughts frankly	300
☐ reveal that ~	086
☐ review	055
☐ **roll up one's sleeves**	158
☐ **rough it**	301
☐ **rub ~ the wrong way**	188
☐ **rub in ~**	189
☐ **run across ~**	198
☐ **run for ~**	199
☐ **run into ~**	090
☐ **run out of ~**	091
☐ **run up against ~**	092

S

☐ **save one's breath**	288
☐ say ~ one had been holding back from saying	293
☐ say something inappropriate	368
☐ say what another thinks	382
☐ **scratch the surface**	173
☐ search everywhere for ~	213
☐ **Search me.**	128
☐ **see eye to eye**	190
☐ seek election to become ~	199
☐ seem understandable [comprehensive]	059
☐ send out ~	337
☐ serve	335
☐ **serve ~ right**	215
☐ share one's thoughts and feelings with ~	253
☐ **show up**	060
☐ **sign up for ~**	191
☐ **sing another tune**	380
☐ **sink in**	159
☐ **sit in for ~**	259
☐ **six of one and half a dozen of the other**	220
☐ skip a lesson	325
☐ **sleep on it**	381
☐ **slip one's mind**	029
☐ **smell a rat**	333
☐ smooth over ~	251
☐ **snap out of it**	144
☐ **So far, so good.**	236

☐ solve	101
☐ something completely different	394
☐ **sort out ~**	061
☐ **Speak for yourself.**	237
☐ speak in support of ~	260
☐ **spell out ~**	093
☐ **spick and span**	268
☐ **split the bill**	047
☐ spontaneously	346
☐ **stamp out ~**	340
☐ **stand out**	030, 006
☐ **stand up for ~**	062
☐ start	246
☐ start a relationship	012
☐ start something happening	302
☐ **start the ball rolling**	302
☐ stay alert	283
☐ **stay up**	048
☐ **stick one's neck out**	160
☐ **stick up for ~**	260
☐ **stick with ~**	261
☐ **Still waters run deep.**	398
☐ **stop by ~**	094, 071
☐ stop by the side of the road	332
☐ stop doing [saying] it	043
☐ stop functioning	003
☐ stop to deliver ~	082
☐ stop working hard	154
☐ **straight from the horse's mouth**	311
☐ strongly discourage ~	303
☐ study	041
☐ stumble upon ~	198
☐ submit	100
☐ suddenly	105
☐ support the family	132
☐ survive	275

T

☐ take ~ for oneself	183
☐ take ~ freely	183
☐ **take ~ into account**	200
☐ **take ~ with a grain of salt**	201
☐ take a break [vacation]	175
☐ **take a dip**	334
☐ take a risk	160, 178
☐ **take a shortcut**	063
☐ take a shorter route	063
☐ **take advantage of ~**	097, 262
☐ **take care of ~**	098, 087
☐ **take it easy**	031
☐ take out A on B	174

どれだけチェックできた？ 1 ☐ 2 ☐

どれだけチェックできた？ 1 □ 2 □

著者紹介

高橋基治
Motoharu Takahashi

東洋英和女学院大学教授。サンフランシスコ大学大学院修士課程修了（英語教授法）。TOEFL、TOEIC 対策の著書多数。主な著書に『はじめての TOEFL® ITP 文法』（アルク、共著）、『栄光の単語 TOEIC® TEST リスニング編』（スリーエーネットワーク）、『これ、英語でなんて言う？』（中経出版）他多数。

ロバート・ヒルキ
Robert Hilke

企業研修トレーナー。カリフォルニア大学大学院修了（言語学）。TOEIC をはじめとするテスト対策、異文化コミュニケーションのエキスパート。現在、数多くの大企業で国際ビジネスコンサルタントとして社内教育に携わる。英語教育に関する学術誌への寄稿や、TOEIC、TOEFL、GRE 対策教材などの著書多数。

ポール・ワーデン
Paul Wadden

国際基督教大学英語教育課程上級准教授。ヴァーモント大学大学院修了（修辞学）。イリノイ州立大学大学院修了（英語学博士）。著述家・学者。ニューヨーク・タイムズ、ウォール・ストリート・ジャーナル、ワシントン・ポストなど、多数の新聞および雑誌に執筆。TOEIC、TOEFL 対策などの著書も50冊を超える。

聞いて覚える英単語
キクタン
TOEFL® TEST
【イディオム編】

発行日	2011年10月17日（初版） 2014年11月5日（第4刷発行）
著者	高橋基治、ロバート・ヒルキ ポール・ワーデン
編集	アルク文教編集部
英文校正	Peter Branscombe、Owen Schaefer
アートディレクション	細山田 光宣
デザイン	奥山志乃（細山田デザイン事務所）
ナレーション	Greg Dale、Julia Yermakov
音楽制作	H. Akashi
録音・編集	高木弥生（有限会社 ログスタジオ）
CD プレス	株式会社 学研教育出版
DTP	株式会社 秀文社
印刷・製本	図書印刷株式会社
発行者	平本照麿
発行所	株式会社 アルク

〒168-8611　東京都杉並区永福 2-54-12
TEL：03-3327-1101
FAX：03-3327-1300
Email：csss@alc.co.jp
Website：http://www.alc.co.jp/

Printed in Japan
PC：7011076　ISBN：978-4-7574-2027-4